THE JOY OF
roses

THE JOY OF
roses

Nicolien van Doorn

TERRA

Contents

HIPS OF *ROSA CANINA*

1.

2.

'THE QUEEN OF FLOWERS'

3.

4.

Introduction

Roses have absolutely everything a flower needs. The petals are velvety soft and come in almost any colour. The flowers have various shapes—large or small, open or filled, rounded or pointed. Is there any other plant with this much variation in height and width? There are 30 cm crawlers and climbers that scale a roof with ease. With every conceivable height and width in between. This means there is a suitable rose for every garden. And we haven't even mentioned the best thing yet: most roses bloom for months at a time and many roses spread a heavenly scent.

Another huge benefit of roses is that they contain beneficial substances. The fruit, the rose hip, is used to make jams and sauces that are chock full of vitamin C and antioxidants. Rose water can be distilled from some roses, which is used in the perfume and pharmaceutical industries.

So it's no wonder that the rose has been known as the 'Queen of Flowers' for 2500 years. The Greek poet Sappho was the first to call it that. She was referring to the wild rose, which did not look nearly as streamlined as our modern, cultivated roses. Since then, everyone has been in agreement: the rose is the most beautiful of all flowers!

1. *ROSA* 'LOVELY ROMANZA'
2. ROSE HIPS
3. *ROSA* 'APRICOT QUEEN ELIZABETH'
4. *ROSA* 'GRACE'

SYMBOLISM

A flower so popular that it can't escape having all kinds of characteristics attributed to it. One of which is that it is the flower of love. A red rose means passionate love; the mean thorns remind you that the road of love can be bumpy. Several centuries ago, when a young man could not approach his chosen one to declare his love, he could always say how he felt with a rose. If he gave her a red rose, it meant he felt love and yearning. If she received two roses, one red and one white, she was delighted: it meant that his love would last forever.

The symbolism of roses has changed over time. The red rose is still a symbol of love but a yellow rose, which used to be gifted to someone you hated, means the opposite nowadays: friendship and connection. Which makes sense, because if a yellow rose still symbolised hate, there would hardly be any sold at all. We can use social media to let people know how we feel about them much more efficiently.

Many religions also use the rose as a symbol. For the early Christians, the red rose symbolised the five wounds of Christ and the white rose symbolised the virginal purity and innocence of Mary. Although it did take a while before that crystallised out: when early Christians first started converting the pagans in Europe, they viewed the rose as something pagan because our ancestors venerated roses as embodying their gods. The proselytisers tried everything to make the rose disappear and it was only when they saw that their attempts were futile that they chose the path of opportunism in the fourth century and turned it into a symbol of their church. From the eleventh century onwards,

1.

the pope gave a 'golden rose' to individuals or institutions on Laetare Sunday as a token of appreciation, and the rose wreath became a part of the profession of faith.

In the Middle Ages and the Renaissance, the thornless white rose (Mary) and the red rose with five petals (the blood from the five wounds of Christ on the cross) can be seen countless times in manuscripts and in paintings. Images often also show Mary surrounded by rose shrubs. The rose motif was also used in sculpture and ironwork, while writers and poets used it to depict passion.

In 1951, the Socialist International was founded, an organisation of social-democratic and labour parties across the world. The organisation's symbol is a closed right hand holding a rose. The fist represents the struggle needed to achieve social security for all. Two of the members are the

Belgian Parti Socialiste and the Dutch PvdA, which used to have a fist and a rose in their logo.

1. *ROSA* 'GOLDEN SHOWERS'
2. MARTIN SCHONGAUER
   MADONNA OF THE ROSE BOWER (1473)
3. *ROSA* 'MARIA MATHILDA'
4. FORMER PVDA LOGO

2.

3.

4.

SUB ROSA

The rose also symbolises secrecy. That has been the case since ancient times. The Romans hung roses above the dinner table to remind guests that everything said while eating and drinking wine should not leave the room. This is called 'sub rosa' or keeping things 'under the rose'. In the Middle Ages, roses were painted on ceilings of meeting rooms and above the *Stammtisch* of inns. The message was clear: everything said about each other and others stays among us. That also helps understand why five-petalled roses are often used as an ornament on confessionals.

SECRET LANGUAGE

The shape and the colour of the rose also spoke a secret language. Every rose had its own meaning. If you gave or received one that was still a bud, it meant that your love had to remain a secret. A rose that was completely open, meant that your love was at an advanced and mature stage.

The colour of the rose was very versatile. A red rose expressed love and yearning, naturally. A white rose indicated that it was about spiritual rather than physical love. Yellow roses were about betrayal and hate. If your lover gave you one, you knew they suspected you of infidelity.

We can still express many things with the colour of roses. For us, too, red roses represent love and romance: they are the flowers you give to your sweetheart on Valentine's Day. Burgundy roses express mourning and sadness and are often used at funerals. White roses, a symbol of purity, are beloved in bridal bouquets. You can give a bouquet of yellow roses to cheer someone up—an ideal gift when you go on a hospital visit. A bouquet of orange roses expresses sociability and makes a good birthday gift.

In addition to the colours, the number of roses you give or receive also has a meaning. If you get a single rose, you know the giver loves you. A single rose in any other colour means "Thank you!" Two or twelve roses mean mutual love: very appropriate for a marriage proposal. You can give five roses to let someone know you really love them. Six to show you are madly in love. Seven to say you want to stay together forever.

1.

Commemorative roses

Roses are the best flower to commemorate certain events. The American Rose Society pronounced 11 September to be the 'Rose Day of Remembrance'. This day of remembrance is connected to the attacks on the World Trade Center in New York on 11 September 2001. In memory of deceased friends and family members, you can order a bouquet of red roses with a red-white-blue ribbon every year on 11 September. At the 9/11 Memorial Pools, a white rose is placed at the name of a victim of the attacks whose birthday was on that day. On Veterans Day, yellow roses are placed at the 9/11 Memorial.

National flower

The national flower of Bulgaria is the Damask rose (*Rosa damascena*), a flower with a delicate scent harvested in Bulgaria for making rose oil. Other countries that have the rose as their national flower are England, Luxembourg, Slovakia and the Czech Republic. The dog rose (*Rosa canina*) is the national flower in Romania.

2.

War of the Roses

The red-and-white Tudor rose is the national flower emblem of England, but for a long time it was unclear whether it would be a red rose or a white one. From 1455 to 1485, the Houses of Lancaster and York fought bitterly over who should rule England. They both had the rose as their symbol: a white one for York and a red rose for Lancaster. Henry VII of the House of Lancaster won the War of the Roses. Henry's marriage to Elizabeth of York united both houses and it became a red-and-white rose, the 'Tudor rose', symbolising unity between Lancaster and York.

Roses accompanying the deceased

In Roman Antiquity, May was the month in which the dead were commemorated. During the Rosalia (rose festivals), rose wreaths were placed on graves and roses were strewn. Offering roses was a way of wishing the deceased a safe journey to the garden of Venus (or the islands of the blessed), where the souls of the deceased flew around like little cherubs.

The pagan Germans also planted roses on their graves, a custom that was later adopted at many cemeteries in Europe; battlefields can be referred to as a 'rose garden' in various languages. If someone found a white rose on their chair, it was seen as a sign of imminent death.

1. BUDDING *ROSA* 'BLUE GIRL'
2. *ROSA CANINA*

THE JOY OF

roses

THE HISTORY
OF ROSES

The history of roses

Roses existed before we humans did

Roses existed before we humans did. In China and North America, fossil rose petals have been found dating back about 40 million years. They were 'wild' roses, with five (or sometimes four) white or red petals around a tuft of stamens. These ancestors of all roses were only found in the northern hemisphere, in North America, Europe and China. They did not naturally occur south of the equator. If you think of our modern burnet rose, you will get an idea of what such roses must have looked like.

When humans developed many millions of years later into beings whose aesthetic senses make a distinction between beautiful and ugly, the rose became their favourite flower. Roses are grown and revered in many countries. The emperor of China had them in his garden five centuries ago—not just because of their beauty and pleasant scent but especially because the flowers and hips helped with health issues. The ancient Persians and Greeks also used rose oil to fight diseases. In the Middle Ages, wild roses were planted in European monastery gardens. The monks made medicines and fragrances from the dog rose (*Rosa canina*), the sweetbriar rose (*Rosa rubiginosa*) and especially the French rose (*Rosa gallica* 'Officinalis').

SEVENTEENTH CENTURY

A major advance was made In the seventeenth century when cultivators discovered that roses could be propagated by taking cuttings and cross-breeding them. Cultivators were able to double the number of petals. Then the flowers took on different shapes: filled in, quartered, like a wide bowl, slender and tall, and many more. Those extra petals were useful because the more petals there are, the more scent the flower has. That was good news in an age when people were not in the habit of showering every day.

The roses became more and more beautiful. But unfortunately, they were only in bloom for about four weeks. This changed at the end of the eighteenth century when roses were found in China that flowered multiple times a season. These Chinese roses were brought to Europe, where they were crossed with European cultivars, resulting all of a sudden in roses that were flowering until the first night of frost! They were called 'repeat-flowering' roses.

EMPRESS JOSEPHINE

Until the eighteenth century, you could only find roses with pink and white hues in Europe. But the available colours changed with the arrival of the 'Chinese roses', which also came in red and soft yellow. These colourful, repeat-flowering roses became very popular and were in high demand. Their popularity became even more intense when Empress Josephine, Napoleon Bonaparte's first wife, had a rose garden planted at Château de Malmaison around 1800. It had rose varieties from all over the world. From then on, everyone who was anyone wanted a rose garden. So you could say that the Empress Josephine was one of the first influencers. After her death, her collection languished, but her roses were preserved on paper thanks to Josephine's court painter Pierre-Joseph Redouté (1759-1840). He preserved the roses in the garden of Château de Malmaison for posterity in his three-volume book *Les Roses*. Unfortunately, the increased demand for roses had its downsides. Cultivators kept cross-breeding the Chinese roses for so long that the roses became exhausted, began to suffer from ailments and became susceptible to all kinds of diseases and pests. This earned the rose the reputation of being a 'difficult plant'.

PIERRE-JOSEPH REDOUTÉ
ROSA GALLICA

Rosa Gallica Aurelianensis   *La Duchesse d'Orléans.*

P. J. Redouté pinx.   Imprimerie de Remond   Langlois sculp.

1867: MODERN ROSES

In 1867, a French rose grower introduced the first hybrid tea rose, which he called 'La France'. 'La France' marked the birth of the modern rose. The flowers are large, beautifully shaped, fragrant and come in many colours; the plant also has long stems. Further crossings created even more groups, such as the floribundas, shrub roses and groundcover roses. These modern roses were so popular that the sales of 'old roses', as they were now called, declined rapidly.

In the Victorian era (1837-1901), people were mainly interested in the flowers, and not so much in the shrubs those flowers grew on. At the flower shows that were so popular during this period, cultivators competed with each other to see who had produced the largest flower and the most showy colour. Because it was only about the flower for the cultivators, they initially did not mind if the shrub producing those flowers was weak and languishing. Around 1900 that problem too was solved when cultivators discovered that weak roses grew better when they were grafted onto the stem of a strong 'wild' rose.

It wasn't until after the Second World War that modern rose breeders started to consider resistance against disease and pests. The roses became healthier, but now they had little or no fragrance. That changed when cultivators such as David Austin managed to reintroduce the scent into modern roses.

DAVID AUSTIN

In the 1950s and 1960s, repeat-flowering tea hybrids were immensely popular, to the dismay of English rose grower David Austin (1926-2018). He did see the benefits of these modern roses: they flowered for much longer than the old roses of the past and were more resilient to diseases. But he didn't like the fact that they had hardly any scent and he wasn't too keen on their harsh, bright colours either. He came up with the idea of combining the advantages of the historic rose varieties (pastel-coloured and fragrant) with those of modern tea hybrids and floribunda roses (healthy and repeat-flowering). After decades of experimentation, in 1961 he introduced *Rosa* 'Constance Spry', a soft pink rose with large, deeply cupped flowers that have the scent of myrrh. It was the first in a long list of 'English' roses, which became so popular that the gardens of England were soon filled with them—to be followed not long after by the gardens of other countries.

ROSA 'CONSTANCE SPRY'

"AROUND FIFTY FAMILIES WORKED IN HIS NURSERY. FIFTY FAMILIES... NOWADAYS YOU'RE LUCKY IF YOU CAN GET FIVE POLISH WORKERS"

Jacques Verschuren

GREAT-GRANDSON OF ROSE GROWER
HENS VERSCHUREN (1844-1918)

In the area around the Dutch village of Haps (North Brabant), you can find numerous rose nurseries that have 'Verschuren' in the name. And that is no coincidence. All those nurseries were founded by the descendants of rose grower Hens Verschuren.

Hens Verschuren's life story is so interesting that one of his great-grandchildren has plans to "do something with it". Whether that means a biography, Jacques Verschuren doesn't know yet. He does have a thick folder containing everything he has collected about 'grandpa' Hens over the years.

In 1867, Hens was appointed headmaster of the village school in Haps. "His hobby was cultivating roses," says Jacques. "He spent all of his free time in the greenhouse next to his house, experimenting with breeding roses." Hens soon ran out of room in the greenhouse, so in 1875 he set up a small rose nursery. This kept him so busy that his teaching suffered. He received a visit from the education inspector, who had heard that Hens was more interested in roses than in the school and that he even had the schoolchildren working in the nursery! Hens was given a choice: teaching or the roses. "He chose the roses," says Jacques. "His oldest rose dates from 1899. One of his most famous is *Rosa* 'Étoile de Hollande', a climbing hybrid tea rose and one of the few

climbing roses that carries on blooming into late autumn." He takes an old booklet from 1888 from his folder. Called *De Roos* (The Rose), it was written by Hens Verschuren. It is full of information about growing and caring for roses. "I'm going to republish this, complete with an update on everything that happened with the Verschuren roses after Hens," says Jacques. "For example, various Verschuren generations have bred about three hundred varieties in total. A hundred of those roses are in the Roozenhuys garden in Haps. Nobody knows whether the remaining two hundred have survived."

While researching his great-grandfather's life, Jacques discovered that Hens had a social side to him. "He had a few homes built next to the nursery for his employees. Around fifty families worked in his nursery. Fifty families... nowadays you're lucky if you get five Polish workers. Us kids used to work with the roses too; I didn't know any better. These days you'll have a hard time getting three lads from secondary school to come in on a Saturday."

Back to Hens, who renamed his rose nursery H.A. Verschuren & Zonen, because three of his sons had now joined his business too. On 1 May 1918, Jac, Toon and Hens Junior took over the nursery; their father passed away on 19 November

Verschuren Collection

At present, the Verschuren Collection has more than ninety different varieties. They were bred from 1875 by Hens, his sons, grandsons and great-grandsons. Many of those roses have names that commemorate family members, such as Nelly Verschuren, Rosa Verschuren, Dries Verschuren, Maria Verschuren, Mrs Verschuren, Verschuren's Glow, Verschuren's Pink, Verschuren's Liebling and Catharina Pechtold. The collection is housed in the Roozenhuys rose garden in Haps and is marketed under the name Collectie Verschuren.

www.rozencollectieverschuren.nl

of that year. The first rose that Hens's sons introduced to the market was called 'Souvenir de H.A. Verschuren' as a tribute to their father. From 1925 onwards, the company became entitled to call itself a royal supplier, and in 1975 H.A Verschuren & Zonen was officially granted the 'Royal' predicate.

1. *ROSA* 'ÉTOILE DE HOLLANDE'
2. BOOK ENTITLED *'DE ROOS'* (THE ROSE)
3. HENDRIKUS ANTONIE (HENS) VERSCHUREN

THE JOY OF
roses

TYPES OF ROSES

Types of roses

There are now over 30,000 known rose varieties

In the nineteenth century, roses became so popular that rose growers were continuously experimenting with crossing and grafting roses, with the result that there are now over 30,000 known rose varieties. To make sense of this enormous number, roses are classified according to the way they grow—in other words, by their appearance. A shrub rose is called such because it doesn't look like a climbing rose, and a climbing rose is very different from a miniature rose.

Roses can also be classified according to their ancestry. This means a division into Old and Modern roses. Old roses are all roses from before 1867, the year in which a Chinese rose was first crossed with a native European variety to create the first hybrid tea rose or Modern rose.

ROSA 'DAME DE COEUR'

Steven van Dalen, owner of De Wilde rose nursery, prefers to classify roses by growth type rather than ancestry. "The problem with the ancestry is that in Old roses the lines of descent get all mixed up," he explains. "That makes it so unclear that a strict regime doesn't work." He opens a huge book in which the roses are classified by ancestry. "Look, nobody can understand any of this," he says. "As soon as you've read it, you'll already have forgotten it. My customers don't want to know where a rose comes from. What's important to them is the height, the colour, whether the plant can handle being by the driveway or whether it can act as a hedge to keep out the neighbouring cats. That's why I always ask first what they plan to do with their new rose. If they say, 'I want the rose to climb up a tree', or 'I'm looking for a low shrub', I know what they're after. Although the use of roses can also overlap. Grandiflora roses can grow in clusters, so that would make it a floribunda rose. And even a climbing rose isn't always a rose that has to go upwards. *Rosa* 'Compassion' is a good climber, but can also stand alone without you having to lead it up something. So then it would be a shrub."

But well, these are exceptions.

Below, roses are classified by growth patterns. The names alone tell you whether the rose does what you want it to do.

CLASSIFICATION BY GROWTH PATTERN

1. WILD OR BOTANICAL ROSES

All of our cultivated roses are descended from wild roses. Wild roses are extremely hardy: they can grow in poor soil and they don't need a lot of care. If you don't prune them, they grow into dense, thorny shrubs that birds and small animals can shelter in. If the shrubs get a bit too big and wild, you can just cut off a chunk. They are a good choice for nature gardens and public green spaces, and can also be planted as hedges.

Most wild roses have single flowers that pollinators such as bees, bumblebees and hoverflies love. What is more, they produce lots of rose hips in autumn, which make the birds very happy. And you too, of course, because you can use those same rose hips to make jam and chutney. So are there any drawbacks to wild roses? Yes, there are: they flower for about four weeks, which is a lot less than the Modern, continuously flowering roses.

Well-known wild roses are the wrinkled rose (*Rosa rugosa*), the sweet briar (*Rosa rubiginosa*), the French rose (*Rosa gallica*), the mandarin rose (*Rosa moyesii*; from western China, came to Europe in 1894) and *Rosa sericea* f. *pteracantha* (from China, came to Europe in 1890). What's striking about this rose is the 1-2cm large, bright red thorns. The burnet rose (*Rosa spinosissima*) is native to Europe and has violet-black rose hips.

1. MANDARIN ROSE
   (*ROSA MOYESII*)
2. *ROSA SERICEA* F. *PTERACANTHA*
3. BURNET ROSE
   (*ROSA SPINOSISSIMA*)

Roses classified by their growth pattern

1. Wild or botanical roses
2. Grandiflora roses
3. Cluster roses
4. Shrub roses
5. Climbing roses
6. English roses
7. Old or historic roses
8. Rose bushes or park roses
9. Miniature and patio roses
10. Groundcover roses
11. Standard and weeping roses

1.

2.

3.

2. GRANDIFLORA ROSES (HYBRID TEA ROSES)

Grandiflora roses, also known as hybrid tea roses, originated from crossing repeat-flowering Chinese tea roses with other groups. They are compact shrubs that can grow to 70-120cm. They usually have one flower on the end of each stem. These are large, full-bodied flowers that start blooming mid-June and don't stop until well into autumn. With their straight stems and often strong fragrance, they make good cut flowers in a vase. These roses can be found in various shapes and colours.

Popular grandiflora roses are 'Audrey Wilcox', 'Dame de Coeur', 'Just Joey', 'Peace' and 'Queen Elizabeth'.

1. *ROSA* 'JUST JOEY'
2. *ROSA* 'QUEEN ELIZABETH'

1.

2.

1. *ROSA* 'PERLE D'OR'
2. *ROSA* 'SCHNEEWITTCHEN'
   (OR 'ICEBERG')

Polyantha or floribunda?

Polyantha roses are crosses between the *Rosa multiflora* and the repeat-flowering Chinese tea roses. Floribunda roses are crosses between grandiflora roses and *Rosa polyantha*, which is why their flowers are larger.

1.

3. CLUSTER ROSES

If you are looking for a rose that produces a lot of flowers well into autumn, the cluster rose is the right choice for you. There are cluster roses with numerous small flowers (polyanthas) or with a few larger flowers (floribundas). The flowers are in bunches on a stem and can be white, pink, red or yellow. The plants remain as nicely compact shrubs that grow to 40-80cm. There are also low cluster roses that don't get taller than 40cm.

Examples of floribundas: 'Absolutely Fabulous', 'Apricot Nectar', 'Astrid Lindgren', 'Bonica', 'Burgundy Ice', 'Friesia', 'Hot Chocolate', 'Marie Curie', 'Poustinia', 'Prinses Claire van België', 'Schneewittchen' (or 'Iceberg'), 'Sexy Rexy' and 'Valentine Heart'.

Some polyanthas, with smaller flowers: 'Cécile Brünner', 'Crystal Fairy', 'Fairy Dance', 'Fairy King', 'Fairy Princess', 'Fairy Queen', 'Lovely Romanza', 'Lovely Fairy', 'Morsdag', 'Perle d'Or' and 'The Fairy'.

2.

1.

4. SHRUB ROSES

Shrub roses grow taller and spread wider than grandiflora roses and cluster roses. Many shrub roses grow to 1.0-1.5m, but there are some that reach 2m or more, both in height and width. They are a popular choice for larger borders and gardens. Varieties that grow straight are suitable for small gardens and flowering hedges. The larger shrubs such as 'Westerland' can also be used as low climbers against a wall. Examples of shrub roses: 'Jacqueline du Pré', 'Nostalgie', 'Red

Ballerina' and 'Westerland'. And the Austin roses 'Gertrude Jekyll' and 'Golden Celebration'.

Persica or Hulthemia roses

A new group of garden roses was launched in 2015: the *persica* or Hulthemia roses. They are compact shrub roses that were long found in the deserts of the Persian Empire. This 'new' rose has single flowers that attract bees and butterflies. They come in light and dark pink, lilac blue, light yellow or

2.

salmon orange. Typical of the *persica* rose is the dark spot in the middle of the flower. It resembles an eye, so it seems as if the rose is looking at you. The shrub grows to about 60cm and is resistant to the cold in winter and summer droughts. It is suitable as a garden plant, but also fits in a pot or planter on a balcony or patio. Another plus point is that it is a self-cleaning rose. That means that you don't have to dead-head old blooms to extend the blooming period. The plant produces new flowers spontaneously until well into autumn,

followed by attractive rose hips. Ideal for gardeners looking for an 'easy' option.

1. *ROSA* 'GOLDEN CELEBRATION'
2. *ROSA* 'SMILING EYES'

5. CLIMBING ROSES

Climbing roses grow upwards, as the name implies. But they only do that if they are tied and led up something, because they can't attach themselves like an ivy or a creeper can. They should really not be called 'climbing roses', but 'guided roses'—although I think many people won't understand what you mean if you use that term. Climbing roses get at least 2m tall. The more flexible their branches are, the easier it is to fasten them. You can make them grow up an old, bare tree, or over a pergola, rose arch, arbour or obelisk. Climbing roses also do well against a wall, but they then need a trellis to keep them in place. A useful system for the side of a house is a trellis of stainless steel wire, which is almost invisible outside the growing season.

In roses that grow upwards, we distinguish between climbing roses and rambling roses (or 'ramblers' for short). Climbing roses get 3-4m tall at most, so you can have them grow over a freestanding ornament. Some have stiff branches that grow upwards; others have more flexible branches.

Rambling roses (vine roses, ramblers) grow much faster than climbing roses and also get taller. Some stop at a height of 4m, but there are some that reach 20m, so they need a lot of space. Most ramblers only flower once, but do so very abundantly. Their flowers are usually smaller than those of climbing roses. There are also repeat-flowering ramblers, and ramblers with large flowers, such as 'Albertine'. Many ramblers produce a lot of rose hips after flowering.

Well-known ramblers are 'Bobbie James' (10m), 'Kiftsgate' (12m) and 'Seagull' (6m).

Many climbing roses flower throughout the whole summer, but not all of them. The roses 'Dorothy Perkins' (6m) and 'American Pillar' (3m) only flower once, but do so very abundantly. There are also varieties that do well in spots that get less sunlight, such as 'Adelaide d'Orléans', 'New Dawn' and 'Pink Cloud'. The soft pink 'New Dawn' is also very easy to guide up a support.

Continuously flowering ramblers

Over thirty years ago, the English rose grower Chris Warner introduced a novelty: rambling roses that flower multiple times. 'Warm Welcome' (1986), 'Little Rambler' (1995) and 'Open Arms' (1995) were the first, followed by 'Purple Skyliner' and 'Rambling Rosie'. These roses grow to 2-3m and are easy to guide, making them ideal for smaller gardens. Another repeat-flowering rambler rose is 'Ghislaine de Féligonde'. 'New Dreams' and 'Perfume Dreams' from the cultivator Martin Vissers also flower repeatedly.

The German breeding company Rosen Tantau released a Perennial series: 'Perennial Blue', 'Perennial Blush', 'Perennial Domino' and 'Perennial Rosali'. The firm Kordes felt obliged to follow suit and released the Siluetta series: 'Crimson Siluetta', 'Lavender Siluetta', 'Purple Siluetta', 'Romantic Siluetta', 'Sunny Siluetta' and 'Sweet Siluetta'. These are all strong, healthy ramblers that flower multiple times.

ROSA 'PERENNIAL DOMINO'

6. ENGLISH OR AUSTIN ROSES

At the start of the 1960s, the English cultivator David Austin decided to combine the advantages of Old roses with those of Modern roses. By crossing them, he created roses that are known today as 'Austin roses' or 'English roses'. They have the full-bodied flower shapes, colours and wonderful scent of Old roses, but flower throughout the summer. Most varieties become large shrubs; others are suitable as bush roses or climbing roses, or as tub plants for on the balcony or the patio.

A plus point of these roses is that they only need four hours of sun per day instead of the usual six. Do keep in mind that they don't like getting the full brunt of the afternoon sun. The most suitable place is somewhere where they only get direct sunlight in the morning or evening.

But no matter how beautiful they are and how nice they smell, English roses also have some downsides. The flowers are so large and heavy that the young branches bend and can collapse under the weight. Once the branches have grown older and thickened, this problem goes away. Another problem, however, is that while the shrubs are perfectly at home in the mild English climate, many don't do as well in the distinctly harsher Dutch winters. What is more, some English roses don't handle wet conditions very well. If it has rained a lot for a long time, the buds will rot—the petals get stuck together and no longer open. Moreover, many English roses are not resistant to diseases and pests such as mildew and black spot.

1.

4.

Some popular English roses

'The Alnwick Rose'

'Charles Austin'

'Compassion'

'David Austin'

'Darcey Bussell'

'Gertrude Jekyll'

'Heritage'

'Imogen'

'Jubilee Celebration'

'Lady of Shalott'

'Leander'

'Queen of Sweden'

1.

7. OLD OR HISTORIC ROSES

Old or historic roses are cultivated (= bred) rose varieties. Crossing European and Chinese roses allowed varieties to be created that are now called Old or historic roses—a term also covering varieties that already existed. The name 'old' is used because most of these roses already existed before the arrival of the Modern roses in 1867.

Historical roses can be divided into two subcategories: the old roses from Europe that only flower once per year, and the group created from crossings between European and Asian roses that flower until well into autumn.

Historical roses have densely filled and usually wonderfully scented flowers in white, pink and purple colours. When more modern varieties with more pronounced colours such as red, yellow and orange became popular in the twentieth century, the Old roses were in danger of disappearing from gardens. But fans of these roses made sure that many were preserved after all. In recent times, the historical roses with their shrub-like growth, full flower shape and wonderful fragrance have been making something of a comeback. Well-known Old roses are 'Blush Noisette', 'Comte de Chambord', 'Ferdinand Pichard' (with striped flowers), 'Honorine de Brabant', 'Gruss an Aachen', *Rosa chinensis* 'Viridiflora', 'Rose de Rescht', 'Charles de Mills', *Rosa gallica* 'Officinalis', *Rosa gallica* 'Versicolor' (with striped flowers), 'Ulrich Brünner Fils' and 'Zéphirine Drouhin'.

1. *ROSA* 'ROSE DE RESCHT'
2. *ROSA* 'BLUSH NOISETTE'
3. *ROSA* 'FERDINAND PICHARD'

8. ROSE BUSHES OR PARK ROSES

Any Modern rose that doesn't fit into a certain category is called a 'bush rose' or 'park rose'. They are the larger, broader shrub and cluster roses. They are hardy, can grow to 2-3m tall and have many single flowers arranged together in clusters. Almost all bush roses are repeat-flowering.

Bush roses have a lot of plus points. To start with, you can do all kinds of things with them. You can plant large areas with them or make an impenetrable hedge; that's why they are often to be found in municipal parks and borders. You can plant the varieties that grow taller against a fence or use them as a low-growing climbing rose. Bush roses are not very susceptible to diseases, combine well with other plants, do well a bit of shade and require little maintenance.

The following bush roses are very healthy and if you dead-head blooms that have finished flowering, these roses will flower from early in the season until well into autumn: 'Angela', 'Bonica', 'Lavender Dream', 'Pearl Drift', 'Penelope', 'Purple Breeze', 'Rosy Cushion', 'Rush', 'Symphonica', 'Westzeit' and 'White Fleurette'.

ROSA 'LAVENDER DREAM'

9. MINIATURE AND PATIO ROSES

Miniature roses are shrubs that usually don't grow beyond 30-40cm. They are suitable as ground cover, but they also do well in a pot or planter. They have many branches and small flowers arranged together in clusters. Miniature roses were created from 1930 onwards from crossings between short Chinese roses and polyantha roses. Because they were then crossed with many other types of roses, there are miniature roses that look like miniature tea hybrids, miniature moss roses and miniature climbing roses. Some are even available as a standard rose.

Patio roses are a bit bigger than miniature roses. Miniature roses and patio roses flower abundantly and are very suitable for small gardens, planters, tubs and pots.

Examples are 'Chili Clementine', 'Lupo', 'Poppy Rose', 'Riverdance', 'Starlet Melina', 'Sweet Dream' and 'Topolina'.

10. GROUNDCOVER ROSES

Groundcover roses don't grow taller than 50-60cm but can cover more than 1m with their long, flexible stems. They need little maintenance and their branches and leaves can fill entire sections, making them suitable for 'difficult' parts of the garden. After a couple of years, the rose will have covered a slope or flowerbed completely and you won't see weeds there anymore. If you want to prune them (once every four years), use a hedge trimmer to clip them down to 5-15cm from the ground.

Groundcover roses also do well in pots or in hanging baskets. Examples are 'Alcantara', 'Alpenglühen', 'Amber Sun', 'Apfelblüte', 'Aspirin Rose', 'Félicité et Perpétué', 'Fil des Saisons', 'Green Summer', 'Happy Chappy', 'Heidekönigin', 'Heidetraum', 'Innocencia', 'Knirps', 'Larissa', 'Laura Ashley', 'Loredo', 'Magic Meidiland', 'Mirato', 'Neon', 'Pretty in Pink', 'Rosy Cushion', 'Rosy Carpet', 'Schneeflocke', 'Queen Mother', *Rosa pimpinellifolia*', 'Stadt Rom' and 'Tapis Volant'.

An interesting new groundcover rose is *Rosa* 'Crewcreep' syn. 'Centre Stage' from Chris Warner. The rose nursery Jac. Verschuren-Pechtold has started growing this rose in 2024, initially in small numbers.

11. STANDARD AND WEEPING ROSES

A standard rose is a normal rose that is grafted at eye level onto the rootstock of a wild variety, such as *Rosa canina* or *Rosa rugosa*. The rootstock doesn't grow taller anymore but does get thicker every year. The roses grafted onto the rootstock are varieties bred by people, such as grandiflora roses, cluster roses, miniature and patio roses or historical roses. The taller stems often have climbing roses, which droop down nicely. Standard roses also do well in pots. Examples of standard roses: 'Alcantara', 'Annapurna', 'Global Hit', 'Heilige Elisabeth', 'Ingrid Bergman', 'Leonardo da Vinci', 'Princesse Charlène de Monaco', 'Schneewittchen', 'The Fairy' and 'Virgo'.

When a climbing rose with long, flexible branches is grafted onto a 140cm tall rootstock, you get a weeping rose. The twigs have nothing to hold onto, so they droop and this creates the weeping shape. Make sure the rose is anchored to a sturdy pole. Well-known weeping roses, often planted in cemeteries, are: 'Albéric Barbier', 'Charmant', 'Excelsa', 'Jasmina' and 'Satina'.

ROSA 'LEONARDO DA VINCI'

"WE PROPAGATE THE ROSES THAT THE PLANT BREEDERS CREATED. WE'RE THE LAST LINK IN THE BREEDING PROCESS"

Steven van Dalen

OWNER OF THE ROSE NURSERY
DE WILDE IN EMPE

Say "rose nursery" and you are saying "De Wilde". Everyone who has anything to do with roses knows the Zutphen nursery, which incidentally is no longer located in Zutphen. In October 2022, Steven van Dalen, owner of De Wilde, sold the land to the municipality of Zutphen. "I had to go, as Zutphen needed the land for building houses. This has been going on for years and the next step would have been expropriation." He deliberately went looking for a location close by, and now grows his garden roses in the outskirts of Empe, a village west of Zutphen. What has also changed is that he no longer sells cut flowers. "I had to make a choice: do I keep doing everything or not? I decided to make things a bit easier for myself. After all, I also sell garden roses online and the nursery is open on Saturdays."

The rose nursery De Wilde has been in business for over a hundred years, although that isn't actually true for the Zutphen location. "My grandfather started growing vegetables in Zutphen in the 1960s," says Steven. "After that, my father grew conifers, heather plants, cut chrysanthemums and strawberries. In the early 1990s he and I started selling cut roses." Meanwhile, in Bussum, there was the De Wilde nursery, which had been growing garden roses since 1921. "When they had to leave Bussum in 2003, we

merged to become one company. De Wilde is a known name in the world of roses, so we kept that name." Steven grew into the job slowly. "Around 1998, my parents started cutting back their involvement. And now with the move to Empe, we're entering another new phase."

His clients can choose from more than 800 varieties of garden roses, the majority of which are sold via the Internet. "Some people know exactly which rose they want," says Steven, "but most come here with a question. They want to know what rose can climb in a tree or up a trellis. Or what rose is suitable as a hedge, because they have trouble with the neighbour's cats. These types of questions are best put to a specialist grower. Garden centres don't have that expertise anymore. They don't need it, because garden centres have become a place for fun-shopping. Consumers go there for a lounge set and pick up a potted rose on the way."

De Wilde buys cuttings and grafted roses, which he then grows for sale. "We propagate the roses that the plant breeders created. We're the last link in the breeding process." When determining which roses he sells and which not, Steven asks himself the question: What does it add? "If I have a hundred roses, what do I need a hundred and twenty for? And why do I need yellow roses if they don't sell? I used

to throw away unsold roses. But when the economy is in recession you have to make different choices, or you'll go under. Everything has become so expensive that I need to sell all my roses. The question is: can I please everyone with what I do? Because you want everyone to be able to find something they want at your place. The trick is not to grow all varieties, because that costs money. Compare it to a restaurant that offers ten types of fish and ten types of meat: before you know it, you'll be swamped by your stock. I know roughly what percentage I sell, and I buy my roses based on that. But I also want unusual varieties in the assortment Beautiful purple roses such as 'Indigoletta' or 'Rhapsody in Blue'. And my personal favourites, of course, such as 'Compassion' and 'Guirlande d'Amour', both climbers." About two thousand rose varieties are sold in the

1. PUTTING TOGETHER ORDERS FOR SHIPPING
2. *ROSA* 'BONICA'
3. *ROSA* 'INGRID BERGMAN'

Netherlands. "Every year, breeders come up with about fifty new varieties," says Steven. "But it can take ten years before people ask for that new rose. They prefer a variety that they know, such as 'Bonica', 'Ingrid Bergman' or 'The Fairy'. It's very difficult for a new rose to get included in that list; it's almost impossible to publicise the rose. What also doesn't help is that gardeners learn about maybe five varieties during their training, and that's it. Even roses that have been tested for years and win prizes, such as Excellence roses, aren't covered. Those award ceremonies are a snapshot; I don't even pay attention to them. And people aren't interested in that kind of thing. Most have a postage-stamp garden and want roses that are pink, red and hardy. Another thing is that people have different ideas about gardening than in the past. That changes over time. Nowadays many people don't enjoy gardening, don't have the time, or both." According to him, the number of rose growers is rapidly declining. "Twenty years ago, there were about eighty growers; ten years ago there were fifty—and of those about fifteen are left. The fewer growers there are, the more the product range shrinks. If a grower doesn't make any sales of a certain rose for two years, they'll stop growing it. The variety will still exist but is no longer being sold. You can't keep growing a rose indefinitely. You choose a certain product range that is profitable. This is good because you are left with the strong varieties, the varieties that are in demand."

What should people look out for when buying a rose? "That the rose isn't susceptible to diseases. That it was organically grown, is repeat-flowering and has a fragrance. The colour of the flower is also important, of course. People usually choose pink, white or red. In that order. Yellow is a long way behind those three. Yellow is a tough colour; you have to make sure your garden can take it."

When it comes to repeat flowering and fragrance, you're soon talking about English roses, which were developed by David Austin starting in the 1960s. "The benefits of English roses are that they are repeat-flowering, smell nice and have attractive leaves," Steven says, summarising. "But they also have disadvantages. They have weak branches, the flower buds droop and they are susceptible to mildew. People say that has improved since 2000, but that's not the case.

Pyrethrin and Rosacur

Pyrethrin is an insecticide of natural origins that is certified for use in organic farming. It consists of various active ingredients, so that the insects can't develop resistance to the product. It breaks down quickly and has a minimal environmental impact. There are also downsides: in addition to the harmful ones, Pyrethrin also kills the useful insects. And it only works for a short interval, so it needs to be applied regularly. Rosacur contains the active ingredient tebuconazole, which is effective against fungal diseases such as black spot, mildew and rust. Tebuconazole has a relatively low acute toxicity.

Trademarks and plant breeders' rights

Trademarks protect the rose's name for ten years and can then be extended indefinitely. Registration in the trademark register gives a grower the right to prohibit others from using the trademark. But other people can still market the same rose under a different name. Trademarks are indicated by an R (in a circle) or by adding TM after the name of the rose. The ® symbol stands for 'registered trademark', the ™ symbol comes from the USA and stands for 'trademark'.

If a breeder has been cross-breeding roses for years and has finally created the perfect new rose, they patent it. Other breeders who want to include this rose in their product range and propagate it must pay the breeder who 'made' the rose a specified amount (licence fee). The plant breeders' rights for roses apply for 25 years, during which others can only propagate the rose if they have a licence contract with the holder of that plant breeder's right. A plant breeders' right is indicated by stating PBR (Plant Breeders' Right) after the name.

English roses have the sensitive leaves of Old roses, which fungi thrive on."
There's that word: 'fungi'. It makes you wonder how a nursery like De Wilde deals with the problem. "Our roses aren't organic," Steven admits. "It's difficult to grow roses organically for technical reasons. To keep them healthy, you need to make sure they get the right nutrients, or they won't turn out well. Our roses are fertilised organically, but that washes out easily in our sandy soil. Once a year, in spring, I use Osmocote. That's as organic as possible."
What is more, in the case of grafted roses, the grower doesn't know how the rootstock was treated. "If the rootstock wasn't grown organically, the rose isn't organic. But that's almost impossible to trace." He sprays the plants as little as possible.

"There are fewer and fewer of these products anyway, and organic products are just as effective. We use Pyrethrum for lice and Rosacur for fungi."

ROSE NURSERY DE WILDE
Ganzekolk 7, 7399 AK Empe, Netherlands
Opening hours Friday and Saturday from 09:00 to 17:30.
www.dewilde.nl

03

THE JOY OF

roses

CHOOSING
ROSES

JOHN WILLIAM WATERHOUSE
THE SOUL OF THE ROSE (1908)

'YOU'LL ALWAYS FIND A ROSE THAT SUITS YOU'

Choosing roses

Fortunately, there are roses of all shapes and sizes

There was a time when I gave roses a wide berth. There were so many, and so many kept getting added, that I never knew which one to choose. It's hard because when buying a rose you really need to know whether it is a wild rose, an English rose, a shrub rose, a musk rose, a climbing rose, a cluster rose, a grandiflora rose or some other kind. After all, you want to know how and when it has to be fed and pruned.

I now know what to pay attention to when choosing a rose. First of all the size, of course. You can't plant a rambling rose in a tiny garden, although nowadays there are ramblers that stay a bit smaller in size. Once this enthusiastic climber shoots up, you won't have room for a garden table and matching chairs. You'll also get into arguments with the neighbours because this rambler won't let a little thing like a dividing fence stop it.

So you need to check how much space you've got. Fortunately, there are roses of all shapes and sizes, from 30cm miniature roses to metres-high climbers. So you can always find one that fits in your garden or on your patio. If you have a tiny garden, you can consider groundcover roses, miniature roses or roses in pots. You can also go for a vertical element by having a rose climb up against a wall or fence. You should then choose one that doesn't get out of hand and grow beyond a metre or two. If you have a bit more space, you can consider a standard rose. They are useful because other plants can grow underneath them. A regular-sized garden will also have room for shrub roses. They grow to between 50cm and 2m tall.

If you are looking for a rose, there are various things you should pay attention to. We have listed ten aspects below.

1. BOUQUET OF ROSES FROM THE GARDEN: *ROSA* 'BETTY PRIOR', TEQUILA', 'TOM TOM', 'AMBER SUN', 'ROBUSTA', 'STADT ROM', 'LILI MARLEEN' AND 'FRAGRANT DELIGHT'

2. FROM LEFT TO RIGHT: *ROSA* 'AMERICAN PILLAR', 'DORTMUND', 'WESTERLAND' AND 'SAMARITAN'

FLOWER

When choosing a rose you probably first look at the most striking part of the plant, which is the flower. Some roses have large, full-bodied flowers. But there are also flowers that look like one a child would draw: a yellow heart with five white or pink petals around it. For centuries, all roses were like the child's drawing. But once breeders discovered that roses can be crossed, they were unstoppable. First, they doubled the number of petals by converting stamens into petals. Then the roses were 'redesigned' to give different flower shapes: open cup, tightly packed, quartered, etcetera. You can compare the situation to dogs, where both the Saint Bernard and the chihuahua are descended from the grey wolf, as is everything in between.

In the nineteenth and twentieth centuries rose lovers were mainly focused on the flowers: the bigger and more colourful, the better! Large flowers are still popular, but nowadays there is a growing demand for wild roses. With their open flowers, these are the roses that bees, bumblebees and other insects get the most benefit from. The insects can get inside the flower easily, which cannot be said for roses with twenty, forty or even a hundred petals.

Shapes the flowers can have

— **Single:** the flowers have five (sometimes four) petals.
— **Semi-full:** twenty or more petals.
— **Full:** a lot of petals, sometimes up to a hundred.
— **Flat or open:** these flowers have five petals, or are semi-filled with distinctive flat petals. Mainly found in wild roses.
— **Chalices:** the flower is open, stamen can be seen in the heart. They can be single, semi-full, full or double-full. The petals are bent outwards.
— **Pointed:** the flowers have pointed buds. They can be semi-full or full and have a prominent heart. Typical of grandiflora roses.
— **Cups:** the flower has a cup shape.
— **Urns:** a flower with a rounded shape and a flat top. They can be semi-full, full or double-full. Found in grandiflora roses.
— **Round:** a flower with a closed, round shape. The flower is full or double-full with overlapping petals of equal size.
— **Rosette:** a large flower that is full or double-full and often has a flat shape with many overlapping petals of varying sizes.
— **Quartered:** a flower with many petals of varying sizes, grouped into four sections. The flower is often flat and full or double-full.
— **Pompon:** the flowers are small and round, and are full or double-full with many petals that are all the same size.

1. *ROSA* 'SWEET PRETTY' (SINGLE)
2. *ROSA* 'LEERSUM 700' (HALF-FILLED)
3. *ROSA* 'MME MARIE CURIE' (FILLED)
4. *ROSA* 'PRETTY SNOW' (FLAT OR OPEN)
5. *ROSA* 'ALIBABA' (GOBLET SHAPED)
6. *ROSA* 'DOUBLE DELIGHT' (POINTED)

7. *ROSA* 'BROTHER CADFAEL' (BOWL-SHAPED)
8. *ROSA* 'BARKAROLE' (URN-SHAPED)
9. *ROSA* 'CLAIRE AUSTIN' (ROUND)
10. *ROSA* 'FELICIA' (ROSETTE)
11. *ROSA* 'GIARDINA' (QUARTERED)
12. *ROSA* 'WHITE FAIRY' (POMPOM)

LEAF

The foliage of a rose is important, because it tells you whether the shrub is healthy. So don't just look at the flowers, but also at the leaves. They should be green, not yellow, brown or black. The leaves can be hairless (glossy) or have felt-like hairs (matt). The plant uses its leaves to collect energy. The more leaves a rose has, the more energy it has to produce flowers.

FLOWERING PERIOD

An important question when looking for a rose is: do I want one that starts flowering abundantly in May or June, but stops after four weeks? Or would I rather have one that flowers less abundantly but keeps going until well into the autumn?

Why is there such a difference between roses in their flowering periods? To find out, we need to go back in time briefly. Until about two hundred years ago, gardens were full of roses that flowered for just four weeks. Then they were finished flowering, and the rose looked like a normal green shrub until the first night of frost. This changed when Colonel Parsons brought four roses back from China (*Rosa chinensis*) to England in 1793. They weren't particularly special roses, but they had something that no other rose had until then: they continued to flower all summer!

Rose growers pounced on the Chinese rose and crossed it with European roses to extend the flowering period of European roses as well. An additional advantage was that the shrub became more compact and no longer looked like a wild bramble bush. Rose expert Marnix Bakker sees this as a rather unfortunate development: "Breeders select the wrong things. A rose is a plant that flowers for four weeks and then stops. Repeat-flowering roses have a gene defect that keeps them flowering. People who want a repeat-flowering rose really want a rose that's broken."

3.

Single-flowering and repeat-flowering roses

Examples of single-flowering roses are the alba roses, Boursault roses, centifolia roses, Damask roses, Gallica roses and moss roses.

Repeat-flowering roses are the Bourbon roses, Chinese roses, remontant roses, noisette roses, Portland roses and grandiflora roses (tea hybrids).

Continuous-blooming roses produce shoots that lead to almost uninterrupted flowering during the season. In repeat-blooming roses, the plant forms new shoots from below, which make it flower again a few weeks later.

1. LEAVES OF THE REDLEAF ROSE
   (*ROSA GLAUCA*)
2. *ROSA* 'AUGUSTA LUISE'
3. *ROSA* 'CHAPEAU DE NAPOLÉON'

1.

3.

Blue or black roses?

Blue roses don't exist, although breeders are doing their very best to find them. The colour blue is formed by certain pigments which until now have not been found in any rose. There are roses with the word 'blue' in their name, such as 'Blue Girl', 'Blue Monday', 'Blue Moon', 'Blue River' and 'Rhapsody in Blue'. But these are roses that are closer to purple or lilac. There aren't any black roses either, and there never will be. Although breeders try to get as close to black as possible, with roses like 'Black Baccara', 'Pretty Black', 'Black Magic' and 'Eddy Mitchell'. But the colour black absorbs so much heat and light that a black flower would burn. That's why the colour black only occurs in shade plants.

COLOUR

Flower colours are not designed to brighten up living rooms or decorate gardens; they are designed to attract insects, birds and other fauna. The more colours a garden has, the more pollinators will be drawn to it. The reason why there is so much variation in the colour of flowers is because insects have their preferences.

Plants know this. But what plants don't know is that people love flower colours just as much as bees and butterflies. Roses are great from that point of view because, aside from blue and black, they come in every conceivable colour. Some even have more than one colour, are striped or start with orange buds that change into pink petals.

Having roses in almost all colours is a new development from the past couple of centuries. Before then, Europeans had to be content with wild roses, which were white or pink. They only learned about red roses around 1800, with the arrival of the 'Chinese rose'. Then came the tea rose, which introduced the soft yellow varieties. Bright yellow and orange roses were added to the assortment around 1900, when the Frenchman Joseph Pernet-Ducher created a deep yellow rose after twenty years of experimenting. Once roses contained natural red, pink, yellow and orange pigments, breeders also managed to create various shades of purple.

A new colour can be created in various ways. Different-coloured varieties can be crossed with one another. This gives seedlings that look a lot like one of the parents, or just a little bit, or not at all. Sometimes a spontaneous mutation makes a different colour appear. If the breeder sees that, they select that plant and cultivate it as a separate variety. The more the genetic material is mixed, the more possibilities for new colours are created.

There is only one green rose, *Rosa chinensis* 'Viridiflora'. Its green sepals are fused into a kind of flower. The 'flowers' sometimes have reddish brown shades. The rose has no scent but does bloom from May to October. When the flower has finished blooming, it remains on the shrub for a long time. This makes it a popular rose among flower arrangers.

1. *ROSA CHINENSIS* 'VIRIDIFLORA'
2. *ROSA* 'PLAISANTERIE'
3. *ROSA* 'BLUE GIRL'
4. *ROSA* 'ORANGES AND LEMONS'

SCENT

Not everyone is equally sensitive to fragrance, because this is something personal. But a rose... I think there are very few people who could walk past one without sticking their nose into the flower. When it comes to fragrance there are three types of roses: strongly scented, lightly scented and with virtually no scent. The intensity depends on the variety: some roses are more fragrant than others. The more petals, the stronger the scent. The time of day also plays a role. A rose that doesn't have much scent in the morning can be intoxicating in the evening. The weather is also important: the hotter it is and the less windy, the stronger the fragrance. The colour also says something about the scent. Dark red roses are less fragrant than light yellow and pink roses. Even the soil type has an influence: roses are more fragrant when grown in heavy soil than in poor soil.

Essential oils

Plants, including roses, don't have scents to please us. They do it to attract bees, bumblebees, butterflies and other insects, in the hope that they will pollinate the plant. That's why a half-opened flower, which is ready to get pollinated, usually smells more intense than a fully opened flower. Roses get their scent thanks to essential oils which are produced by glands in the petals. When the oils evaporate, we perceive it as a fragrance. The more petals, the more intense the scent. That's why roses with full blooms spread a stronger scent than wild roses, which only have five petals. The stamens and the carpels also emit a scent, and sometimes even the leaves. The leaves of the primula rose (*Rosa primula*) smell of incense, while the flower buds and leaves of moss roses have a herbal, resinous scent. And if you crush the leaves of the sweetbriar rose (*Rosa rubiginosa*), you smell green apples.

If you have a particularly refined sense of smell, you would be able to distinguish more than twenty-five different scents. Just like with wine, they are described using terms such as sultry, fruity, herbal, spicy or musty. Or, even more specifically: citrus, vanilla, mowed grass, cinnamon, raspberries or pineapple.

The development of rose scents

Until the end of the eighteenth century, only wild roses—which do not have much scent—were grown in Europe. That changed when the first roses were brought to Europe from China. These roses not only bloomed for much longer but also smelled like fruits. Many new scents were created by crossing different roses. This is the reason why Old roses

Differences

Why is it that your mother likes the scent of a particular rose, while you don't like it at all? That's because the nose is not symmetric: the left and right halves perceive a scent in different ways.

(such as gallica, Damask, alba, Portland, centifolia, moss and rugosa roses) have such a nice scent. It's no coincidence that rose oil is made from Damask roses.

Unfortunately, breeders from the nineteenth century onwards were mainly focused on the colour and shape of the flower. They were the most important aspects and the fragrance was a supporting element at best.

Breeding roses with a strong scent is not as easy as you would think. This is because scent is a non-dominant trait. If you cross two highly fragrant roses, the seedlings may have no scent. And if the scent pops up in a later generation, it could be completely different from that of its 'ancestors'. Another factor is that rose breeders have more on their mind than just producing a fragrance. Besides scent, they are focused on the shape and colour of the flower, the shape of the shrub, longevity, sensitivity to frost, resistance to disease and much more. But because nowadays we want roses that don't just have beautiful flowers but also smell nice, there are now breeders working on a breeding programme that focuses on healthy roses with a strong scent.

Some highly fragrant roses

— 'Annapurna'
— 'Bobby James'
— 'Boscobel'
— 'Charles de Mills'
— 'Clarence House'
— 'Compassion'
— 'Darcey Bussell'
— 'Double Delight'
— 'Friesia'
— 'Für Elise'
— 'Gertrude Jekyll'
— 'Golden Celebration'
— 'Guirlande d'Amour'
— 'Lavender Dream'
— 'Little White Pet'
— 'Madame Alfred Carrière'
— 'Princess Alexandra of Kent'
— 'Rhapsody in Blue'
— 'Roseraie de l'Hay'
— 'Tequila Gold'
— 'Winschoten'
— 'Wollerton Old Hall'

1. *ROSA* 'WINSCHOTEN'
2. *ROSA* 'GERTRUDE JEKYLL'
3. *ROSA* 'ROSERAIE DE L'HAY'
4. *ROSA* 'CHARLES DE MILLS'

SOIL TYPE AND LOCATION

Once you've decided what your new rose should look like and what scent it should have, an important question remains: where will you plant your rose? What type of soil does your garden have? Can the rose handle that? And how much sun does it need?

As for the soil type, I can reassure you: roses are not picky. They just don't like acidic soil so much. And they might have a hard time in spots that are very wet or very dry. The best soil type for roses is fertile soil that drains well. Loam and light clay are ideal, but they also do well in sand and heavy clay. As for the sun, roses love sun and light. That's why you should choose a spot where the rose gets four or five hours of sun a day—but make sure it won't be standing in the bright afternoon sun for hours on end. Many roses can also handle semi-shade, but won't bloom so enthusiastically then.

DISEASE RESISTANCE

Of course you also want to know how robust your future rose is. What is the likelihood that it will suffer from diseases and pests? In short, how much time will you have to spend on maintenance? I put these questions to a rose expert. His answer was that you can't say of any rose that nothing will ever go wrong with it. "But doesn't that apply to all plants, animals and people?" he added. "Have you ever met anyone who has never been ill?"

Despite that, there is something to be said on the subject. The roses that are least bothered by annoying fungi, such as black spot and mildew, are the wild roses. There are also roses that are so strong they just keep growing and blooming after a fungi attack (see page 163-165).

THORNS OR SPINES

No roses without thorns, the saying goes. Botanically speaking, a rose doesn't have thorns, but spines.

The difference between thorns and spines is that you can break spines off a branch without damaging it, whereas a thorn is fused to the branch, so you damage the branch if you break off the thorn. Simply put, spines grow on the surface of the stem, the leaf stalk and the flowering stem, while thorns grow from the core.

The rose's thorns (to use the usual term) can be shaped like a hook or a needle. People used to think that they were meant to protect the flowers from getting picked, but that's not the case. The thorns protect the shrub itself, not the flowers. Thanks to the thorns, herbivorous animals think twice before sinking their teeth into the succulent stems. The rose also uses its thorns to attach itself to other plants, so it can grow straight up towards the sun without falling over.

The most spectacular thorns can be found on the wild rose *Rosa sericea* subsp. *omeiensis* f. *pteracantha* 'Atrosanguinea'. They are blood-red, flat, 3cm-wide thorns that look like long wings stuck to the stems. The burnet rose is covered in prickly thorns, both long and short, while those on the stems and buds of the moss rose 'William Lobb' are soft and hairy.

1. *ROSA* 'GHISLAINE DE FÉLIGONDE'
2. *ROSA* 'DORTMUND'
3. *ROSA* 'ESPRESSO'
4. *ROSA RUGOSA*
5. *ROSA* 'WILLIAM LOBB'
6. *ROSA SERICEA* SUBSP. *OMEIENSIS* F. *PTERACANTHA*
7. *ROSA* 'JAMES GALWAY'

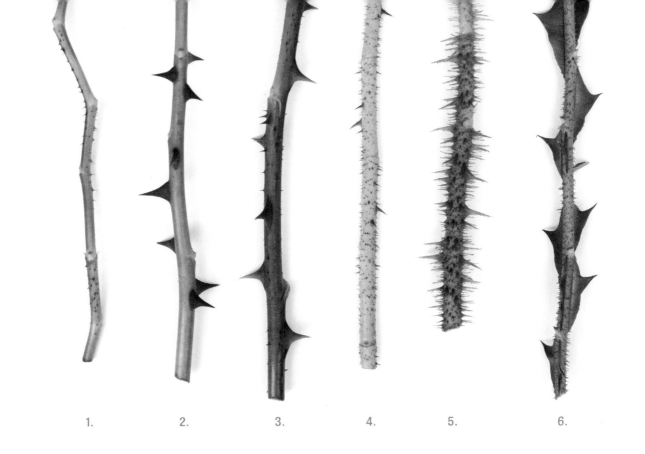

1.   2.   3.   4.   5.   6.

Almost no thorns

All roses have thorns. However, there are a few roses that have very small thorns or very few thorns due to a spontaneous mutation:

— 'Aimée Vibert'
— 'Bleu Magenta'
— 'Blush Noisette'
— 'Climbing Iceberg'
— 'Ghislaine de Féligonde'
— 'Goldfinch'
— 'James Galway'
— 'Kathleen Harrop'
— 'Lady Banks' (banksiae 'Lutea')
— 'Lykkefund'
— 'Madame Alfred Carrière'
— 'Neige d'Avril'
— 'Souvenir du Docteur Jamain'
— 'Veilchenblau'
— 'Zéphirine Drouhin'

**Websites that can help you choose
and buy a rose**
www.helpmefind.com/roses
www.plantenkwekerijen.be/nederlandserozen.html
www.plantenkwekerijen.be/belgischerozenkw.html
www.bierkreek.nl
www.rhs.org.uk/plants/roses/choosing-the-best

POT OR BARE ROOTS

Once you've made a choice, you have to decide whether you want to buy a potted rose or one with bare roots. When you're in a nursery or garden centre, don't just grab the first pot you see. First, check what the rose looks like. If the stem is surrounded by lichen and weeds, you know that the plant has been stuck in that pot for a long time. Also check if it is deeply rooted. Turn the pot upside down and carefully remove the rose. If you see a sturdy, not too dry clump with roots everywhere, you are OK adding the plant to your shopping trolley.

From November to the end of March you will find roses for sale with bare roots. These are roses that have been uprooted directly from the field. The roots are bare without any soil covering them. These plants cost less than potted roses because less work, time and material went into them. When buying the plant, make sure that it has at least three well-formed branches, each at least 40cm long. It also needs to have enough roots, and they must not be dried out (see also page 148).

1. A WELL-ROOTED ROOT BALL
2. ROSE WITH BARE ROOTS

ROSE HIPS

The rose hip looks like a fruit, but it is a false fruit, like the strawberry and the fig. After blooming, when the sepals have fallen off, the flower base grows into a rose hip. Whether the rose hip is red, orange, yellow, brown, purple or black depends on the variety. The shape varies from round or long and thin to bottle-shaped. The rose hips of *Rosa roxburghii* have a particularly unusual shape; they look like chestnuts with their prickly shell. Within the rose hip are yellowish-white, hard seeds. All roses get hips, but every time a flower that has finished blooming is removed, that also means the end of a potential rose hip. If you leave the flowers, they will naturally turn into rose hips.

Rose hips have a lot of nutrients with medicinal properties. In addition to a lot of vitamin C, they also have vitamins A, E and K, as well as various B vitamins and minerals such as calcium, iron, magnesium and potassium. They are also a source of bioflavonoids, antioxidants and pectin. So it is not surprising that they've been used to treat conditions such as colds, the flu, infections, inflammations and digestive problems for centuries.

Rose hips are also used in skin products because of their high vitamin content and antioxidants. Rose hip oil in particular is known for its nourishing properties. The oil is used for treating skin problems such as acne, scars and wrinkles. It is said to rejuvenate the skin and improve elasticity.

In addition to being healthy and beneficial, many rose hips taste nice too. They can be eaten raw, but taste better without the hard shell and seeds. You can use them to make jam, syrup or chutney. And if you dry them, they can go into the teapot. Rose hips are also used in flower arrangements or as an autumnal table decoration.

Roses with decorative hips

Not all roses have attractive fruits. It is mainly the wild roses and shrub and bush roses whose rose hips stand out, along with the crossings with wild roses, such as the 'Pavement' roses with extra large hips. Examples are 'Pierette Pavement' and 'Scarlet Pavement'. Other roses with attractive large hips are the wrinkled rose (*Rosa rugosa*) and rugosa hybrids. What's unusual about rugosas is that the plants can have flowers and hips at the same time. This is also the case in 'Jam-a-Licious', from Jan Spek Roses, which is grown specifically for the hips. Some striking cultivars are 'Blanc

Double de Coubert', 'Fru Dagmar Hastrup', 'Georg Ruf', 'Hansa', 'Jens Munk', 'Roseraie de l'Hay' and 'Rubra'. A rose with very pretty rose hips is *Rosa moyesii* and its cultivar, *Rosa moyesii* 'Geranium'. Its bottle-shaped hips turn from green to yellow to orange to red. *Rosa nitida* has orange-red hips and is even prettier in the autumn with its reddish brown leaves. The hips of the sweetbriar rose (*Rosa rubiginosa*) and the dog rose (*Rosa canina*) are orange-red. The burnet rose (*Rosa spinosissima* or *Rosa pimpinellifolia*) has dark purple, almost black hips. *Rosa pendulina* 'Bourgogne' gets small, red, pear-shaped rose hips after it finishes flowering.

Cultivated (rather than wild) roses with many or unusual hips

The rambling rose *Rosa filipes* 'Kiftsgate' bears large clusters of orange-red hips.

The shrub rose 'Erfurt' has large orange-coloured rose hips. The climbing rose 'Francis E. Lester' produces a lot of hips in the autumn. This rose has a strong scent and is suitable for flower arrangements.

Moschata hybrids such as 'Ballerina', 'Plaisanterie', 'Pink Magic' and 'Sibelius' grow lots of decorative hips. They are usually too small and too hard to use in cooking and birds don't really like them either, but they remain attractive for a long time in bouquets and flower arrangements.

1. WRINKLED ROSE WITH FROST (*ROSA RUGOSA*)
2. EGLANTINE (*ROSA* RUBIGINOSA)
3. WREATH OF VARIOUS ROSE HIPS STRUNG ON STEEL WIRE
4. HIP OF A CHESTNUT ROSE (*ROSA ROXBURGHII*)
5. HIPS OF *ROSA VILLOSA* VAR. *ARDUENNENSIS*
6. HIPS OF *ROSA MOYESII*

Vitamin C

You might have wondered why rose hips contain so much vitamin C. It's not to protect us humans from flu and colds. And the rose itself doesn't benefit either. The fact that rose hips contain so many healthy components shows how ingenious nature is: the aim is to increase the survival chances of the animals that eat the hips and thereby disperse the indigestible rose seeds through their droppings.

1.

2.

3.

4.

Belmonte Arboretum

Many different roses with rose hips can be seen in the Belmonte Arboretum in Wageningen at the end of August and in September. The roses are divided into clear groups. There are clusters with historical and Modern roses, a cluster with groundcover roses, a cluster with the Doorenbos collection and a group with rootstocks.

www.belmontearboretum.nl/en/collectie/top-species/

5.

6.

Bottle

Many rose hips are shaped like a bottle. That's why in Dutch they are called 'bottel', after the English word 'bottle'. If makes you wonder which Dutch person came up with the idea to give these fruits an English name, given that they are called 'hips', and not 'bottles', in English!

"THERE WAS EVEN A WAITING LIST THIS YEAR. THAT'S A NEW DEVELOPMENT"

Emmelie Moerkoert and Eric Hees

ROSE HIP GARDEN DE PUT

On the Amsterdam-Rhine Canal, near Wijk bij Duurstede, you can find the rose hip garden De Put. Here, Emmelie Moerkoert and Eric Hees grow organic rose hips that are processed into food products such as coulis, chutney, jam, wine, beer and bonbons. "If you're looking for anything to do with rose hips, we're the only ones in the Netherlands," says Eric. "There are other growers specialising in rose hips, but they grow them for decoration."

'De Put' (Dutch for *The Well*) is a rather strange name for a garden sitting on a 7m tall mound. But it's an apt name, says Emmelie: "When the canal was built in the 1930s, a dyke was built for dumping the excavated soil. The land behind the dyke naturally becomes a sink. That's why the Wijk bij Duurstede locals call it as 't Stort—*The Dump*."

This is where her parents started growing rose hips. "My father was a fruit grower: cherries, apples and pears. In 1950, this soil depot came up for sale and my parents settled there as a young couple. It contained excavated soil from the Amsterdam-Rhine Canal. There were mounds of sand and clay that had to be mixed. Everything had yet to be developed." She brings out a photo album in which her mother kept track of the garden's construction. A caption under one of the photos says "Wilderness!"

Hans and Topy Moerkoert had intended to grow apples, pears and cherries there. But they never got around to that. "They'd only just settled here when they were approached by the Zwaardemaker firm," says Emmelie. "The firm asked if they wouldn't rather grow rose hips for the Karvan Cévitam brand of syrup. My father was up for the adventure, so my parents planted thousands of *Rosa alpinas* and *Rosa blandas* on 20 hectares of soil between 1951 and 1954. They had to learn everything about growing roses from scratch. Every year, someone came from Limburg to bud graft the roses, day labourers came to prune them and local people picked the hips in August and September." In 1953 the harvest was 747 kilos, just one year later it was already ten times as much and in 1960 the shrubs yielded 31,000 kilos. In that time they regularly received visits from pharmacists, doctors, nurses and other interested parties, Emmelie remembers.

The business flourished until the early 1970s. There was no longer a shortage of vitamin C by then, so the hips became less important as a source of the vitamin. "Also, the economic aspect became more and more important," says Emmelie. "Everything had to be bigger, and as cheap as possible." In 1978, Zwaardemaker uprooted its gardens in the Netherlands and moved production to France. "The

1. ROSE HIPS READY TO BE PICKED
2. THE HARVEST IS COLLECTED IN BASKETS

final blow. Over there they were harvesting with machines, but that's bad for the shrubs." In 1979 it was the turn of the garden in Wijk bij Duurstede. "My parents started their own business then. They farmed two hectares, the rest of the land was rented out. Organic-dynamic farming was up and coming at the time, so they decided to go organic, without artificial fertilisers and pesticides. The hips were sold to Gaiapolis, which used them to make organic jam."

Hans Moerkoert died unexpectedly in 1987. "Eric and I were living in Venezuela. Eric had studied Sociology of Non-Western Regions at Wageningen University and I had a background in nursing. We had intended to stay there for a few years. But after my father's death, we came back. We took over the business and continued the deal with Gaiapolis. Like my parents, we sold the hips direct from the farm—unprocessed, in other words. After we'd done that for a few years, we started looking into other options. We wondered what else we could do with the hips. It was a time in which

consumers were becoming interested in what they were eating and where it came from. Someone gave us the idea to use the rose hips to make wine, and in 1996 we launched the first Canina wine."

In 2008 they bought a pressing machine, which allowed one person to turn a thousand kilos of rose hips into a smooth, highly concentrated puree in just four days. "It's too much work to separate the rose hips by hand," says Eric. "It's much faster with a pressing machine." Arjen Smit, chef at the regional restaurant De Pronckheer in Cothen at the time, used the puree to make a coulis that was so popular that it's still being sold. Lindenhoff, a catering supplier that operates throughout the Netherlands, has had it in their product range for over fifteen years. Enthusiastic buyers include high-end restaurants such as Bolenius in Amsterdam, Héron in Utrecht and De Nieuwe Winkel in Nijmegen. They no longer make jam, says Eric. "It's a shame to sweeten the hips, because rose hips aren't sweet by nature. Hopefully the sugar tax will put an end to sugary products."

Trial fields

During and right after the Second World War, many people were found to have severe vitamin C deficiency. After research showed that rose hips contain high levels of high-quality vitamin C, the government commissioned field trials for rose hips. *Rosa alpina* (synonym *Rosa pendulina*) and *Rosa blanda* in particular looked promising. Around 1940, both roses were tested in field trials in Westbroekpark, a park in The Hague, and in the town of Boskoop. The company Zwaardemaker, which had been producing jam since 1928, had an experimental garden of 2,700 shrubs planted in Maarssen. In 1948, Zwaardemaker launched the syrup Karvan Cévitam. Two years later, they started looking for fruit growers who could take rose hip production further. Those growers were Hans Moerkoert and Topy Piersma.

After the coulis came the chutney, which besides the rose hips also contains apples, plums, spices and apple vinegar. A hairdresser in Utrecht treats his clients' scalps with an essential oil made from rose hips. The Hague brewery Eiber uses it to make 'rose hip beer' and the Utrecht organic soap manufacturer Werfzeep adds hip puree to one of its soaps, while the chocolatier La Fève uses the coulis as a filling in chocolates. "Everything we harvest, we sell," says Emmelie. "There was even a waiting list this year. That's a new development."

But the fact that they are the only ones doing this also has its downsides, according to Eric. "Sometimes it's a bit lonely. We don't have advisers who we can ask how to do something, because we never meet anyone else who has experience with it. We're now considering whether to scale up with three other people, for example by adding eight or ten hectares of adjacent land. We could harvest and process the hips together, have our own brand. With a small picking machine, so we can harvest everything in a couple of days." They're also considering a new product. "A kind of spread. We're exploring what steps we can take. We have quite a few contacts through our catering network. There are a lot of restaurants that want our coulis. That's a sign that you're working on something that's got a future."

THE ACTIVITIES

The De Put rose hip garden works largely with *Rosa alpina*, which can be found on the southern side of the Alps. "Its hips have an extremely high vitamin C content," says Eric. "We have one row of *Rosa blanda*. It has the highest vitamin C content of all, but it's hard to grow. It grows slowly, so you have less production per square metre."

The rose shrubs continue to produce hips for about fifteen years. Every year, a proportion of them are replaced. New shrubs are planted early in the spring, and in June and July Eric cuts off branches. "They go to the Wijnhoven propagator in Limburg. He has thousands, maybe even tens of thousands of *Rosa corymbifera* 'Laxa' shrubs on his land. They are used as the rootstock for bud grafting the roses. Wijnhoven are given a bundle of 500 to 600 branches from us. They take a branch, cut eyes out of it and attach them to the rootstock. Our roses stay there and come back to us in the autumn of the following year. They have lighter soil in Limburg, so we first pot the roses in a sandbox. After that we plant them in their final position, which is never a place where roses have been grown before."

The roses have only a few hips the first year, but they produce

1. EMMELIE AND ERIK PLUCKING HIPS
2. A BUCKET OF ROSE HIPS
3. ROSE HIP JAM MADE USING HIPS FROM 'DE PUT'

a good harvest from the third year onwards. "We fertilise them with organic fertiliser, supplemented with phosphate or lime pellets. We don't irrigate the shrubs as roses can withstand drought well." They prune as late as possible, in March or April. "If you prune early, you leave wounds that fungi can easily get into. In the spring, the shrubs are already growing and the air is dry. So the wounds close up faster and fungi like silver leaf will have less of a chance." The hips are picked from the end of August. "We got 1,200 kilos of hips this year from roughly 850 shrubs. The rose hips go into the freezer, where they are deep-frozen at -18°C. Hips can only be puréed after they have been frozen; otherwise they are too tough. In the months that follow, the hips are taken out in small portions at a time, thawed and rinsed with hot water. Then they go into the pureeing machine. The puree is collected in buckets and gets sent to the companies that use it to make coulis and chutney. Van Woerkom in Nieuwegein pasteurises some of the coulis before it goes into the jars. Others want it unpasteurised in buckets." The final round of mowing follows in October, and then the cycle begins again.

ROSE HIP GARDEN DE PUT
Broekweg 10, 3961 MJ Wijk bij Duurstede, Netherlands
Visitors welcome from May to October, exclusively by appointment.
www.rozenbotteltuindeput.nl

"WE DO THIS IN PART TO PRESERVE THIS PLACE, AS IT'S THE ONLY ORGANIC ROSE HIP GARDEN IN EUROPE"

Jos and Corrie

ROSE HIP PICKERS

Every year, Jos looks forward to the three Saturdays in August and September when the rose hips are picked at De Put. When asked what he likes so much about it, he stretches out his arms and looks around him: "What do you think?" And he's right: this is a special place. Endless fields, apple and pear trees, hens wandering around and long rows of rose shrubs that are full of red, ripe hips. "Everything here is nice," Jos summarises. "The place, Emmelie and Eric, the sociability of the other pickers. And of course we also do this to preserve the place, as it's the only organic rose hip garden in Europe."

Jos has been coming here for fifteen years. "In the past, friends and family of Emmelie and Eric came and did the picking," he says. "They would set up their tents here and camp, but over time fewer and fewer of them came. In 2007 Emmelic and Eric decided they could also ask for volunteers. If you signed up, you got a meal prepared by Arjan Smit of De Pronckheer restaurant in Cothen at the end of the day. We all sat at a long table. The first time, there were almost fifty people! We still get a meal, but it's no longer from De Pronckheer."

That long table with the delicious food is something that 82-year-old Corrie also remembers well. She comes together with Jos from their hometown of Utrecht to De Put every year. Sometimes she also comes outside of harvest time, she says. Simply because it's such a peaceful place. "It's just Emmelie and me then, and we say to each other: Here we are, then, in our kingdom."

1. HIPS OF *ROSA ALPINA*
2. JOS AND CORRIE PICKING ROSE HIPS
3. HARVESTED HIPS IN LARGE BASKETS

THE JOY OF
roses

BUYING
ROSES

Buying roses

Where should you buy your rose?

Buying a rose doesn't have to take a lot of time, because roses are available everywhere. They can be found at rose nurseries of course, at garden centres and florists, or at garden fairs and special garden open days, such as the Boschhoeve in Wolfheze. Even supermarkets and home improvement stores sell roses.

They're available all year round at nurseries and garden centres: flowering in a pot in the summer, and with bare roots in the winter. Florists, supermarkets and home improvement stores only sell roses in the flowering season, when they are at their most attractive. These roses are expensive and were probably sprayed with pesticides or crop protection agents. They are roses that are usually bought on a whim. The good thing about these flowering roses is that you can see what you are buying, which is useful if you're not sure what rose you want. If you do know, you can buy garden roses with bare roots between November and March. They are resting, don't need to spend effort on flowering and have all the time they need to acclimatise.

The easiest way to get hold of roses is through the website of a grower or garden centre. If you order roses this way, all you have to do is wait patiently for the delivery person to come to your door. You can order both roses with bare roots and potted roses online. The plants with bare roots are delivered during their dormant period—between November and March. The photos on the website show you what the rose will look like in six months' time.

If you want to make sure the rose is strong and healthy, it's best to go to a specialist grower. Not only are their roses reliable, they can also give advice and help with choosing the right rose. If you want your future rose to be organically grown, you can go to an organic rose nursery such as De Bierkreek in Biervliet. You don't have to drive all the way to Biervliet in the province of Zeeland though because roses from De Bierkreek are also available online. This nursery also has outlets in Aalbeek, Almere, Amsterdam-Noord, Eldersloo, Eindhoven, Haarlem and Olst in the Netherlands, and in Brussels and Halle in Belgium.

QUALITY LABELS

If you want to know for sure that your future rose is strong and healthy, I'd recommend buying one with a quality label. There are various quality labels, all of which guarantee that the rose in question is of the highest quality.

Excellence Roses (the Netherlands)

The Dutch quality label is called 'Excellence Roses' (previously 'Toproos'). A rose has to clear a lot of hurdles before it is allowed to be called an 'Excellence Rose'. That starts with the breeder who, after years of crossing and selecting, thinks they have created a new rose variety. They send a few of those roses to various inspection gardens. The roses are grown in trial fields for three years, where they have to hold their own without the help of pesticides and winter covers. Four times in each flowering season, they are inspected by judging committees. They give the roses points for aspects such as overall impression, colour and shape of the flower, health and scent. The rose has to pass the inspection at least three times before it's allowed to be called an 'Excellence Rose'. But even then it's not over for the rose, because every five years there is a repeat inspection to see whether the rose still belongs among the top of the product range.

Examples of 'Excellence Roses' are: 'Limona', 'Märchenzauber', 'Midsummersnow', 'Princesse Stéphanie Grande-Duchesse Héritière de Luxembourg', 'Summer of Love' and 'White Valeda'.

BEST-select (Belgium)

The BEST-select quality label is a partnership between twenty Flemish ornamental tree nurseries and the Flanders Research Institute for Agriculture, Fisheries and Food (ILVO). Various new roses resulted from this partnership, including 'André Brichet', 'Archimedes', 'Arte', 'Cera', 'Jacky's Favorite', 'Monia', 'Nero', 'Phaedra', 'Prinses Mathilde' and 'Rivierenhof'.

ADR (Germany)

The strictest inspection system in Europe is Germany's ADR (Allgemeine Deutsche Rosenneuheitenprüfung). For three years and at eleven different locations in Germany, the roses are assessed in terms of foliage health, blossoming period, fragrance, colour and resistance to diseases. During this period, the roses are not treated with chemical crop protection agents and they get no protection against the winter cold. In 2018, it was found that some of the more than four hundred ADR roses at that time no longer met the current requirements for a strong and healthy garden rose. That is why the ADR designation is now only valid for fifteen years. After fifteen years, entrants can withdraw the rose or resubmit it for inspection. If resubmitted, the rose will go through the three-year trial period all over again.

Well-known ADR roses are: 'Bad Birnbach', 'Compassion', 'Dortmund', 'Friesia', 'Guirlande d'Amour', 'Lampion', 'Leonardo da Vinci', 'Nostalgie', 'Rotilia', 'Souvenir de Baden-Baden', 'Tequila' and 'Westzeit'.

AGM (UK)

AGM (Award of Garden Merit) is a quality label assigned by the UK's Royal Horticultural Society to plants that are attractive, strong, healthy and easy.

Some AGM roses are 'A Shropshire Lad', 'Absolutely Fabulous', 'Adélaide d'Orleans', 'Albertine', 'Aloha', 'Compassion', 'Crazy for You', 'Darcey Bussell', 'Diamond', 'Étoile de Hollande', 'Ferdinand Pichard' and 'Ghislaine de Féligonde'.

1. *ROSA* 'HOT ROCK'
2. *ROSA* 'SUMMER OF LOVE'
3. *ROSA* 'JACKY'S FAVORITE'
4. *ROSA* 'GUIRLANDE D'AMOUR'
5. WESTBROEKPARK INSPECTION SITE

Inspection locations

The inspection locations in the Netherlands are
Rosarium in Boskoop, De Rozenhof in Lottum, Rosarium in
Winschoten and Westbroekpark in The Hague.
In Belgium they are the Vrijbroekpark in Mechelen and
Plant Garden 'De Kleine Boerderij' in Merksplas.

"NOT MANY PEOPLE BUY ROSA 'CHECKMATE'. AND WHY DOES NO ONE HAVE THE INCREDIBLY BEAUTIFUL 'LILAC WINE'?"

Hans van Hage

OWNER OF THE ORGANIC ROSE NURSERY DE BIERKREEK
IN BIERVLIET

Among Dutch rose nurseries, one in particular stands out, and that's De Bierkreek in Biervliet, Zeeland. What makes De Bierkreek special is that the roses here have been grown organically for almost a quarter of a century. That means no crop protection agents, no chemical pesticides and no artificial fertilisers. And that's pretty unique, says co-owner Hans van Hage. "When we started, there was one certified organic nursery in Germany. Another one came after us, a small one in former East Germany. The three of us are the only ones in the whole of Europe. There is no one else in the world, as far as I know." Not even in Britain? Hans: "Especially not in Britain; they are too conservative for that. And it's not really a rose country."

If you ask Hans how it all started, he replies with a hilarious story. "In 1999, my wife Marianne and I were in the pub with our friends Eric and Geertje. Marianne said, 'I'd actually like to work with my hands again. A plant nursery maybe.' To which Geertje replied, 'Yes, roses!' To which I said, 'It's my only area of expertise, what with my northern Limburg roots.' Marianne and Geertje in unison: 'But it's got to be organic!' We started drawing what it should look like on the back of a beer mat. Eric had the land and I started calling rose growers: what are the options, is it even possible in Zeeland?

Of course it is, the growers said, it'll be even better on heavy soil than on sandy soil. A week later we ordered 10,000 rootstock units, which we planted in the spring of 1999. We had the first harvest in 2000."

They currently grow between 350 and 400 varieties. That includes varieties that no one else has, which can be scary at times, says Hans. "If we stop growing that variety, it will no longer exist. There are always a few idiots who order such a rare variety, but that's about it. If as grower you decided to continue with such a rose, you'd have to make it very expensive. But we don't like doing that."

ROOTSTOCK

The roses are propagated using cuttings or bud grafting. Cuttings are taken of roses that have their own strong roots. This is done at the organic nursery Dependens in Bennekom, where they are potted in De Bierkreek's own pots and potting compost. When the plants are fully grown, they are shipped to the sales outlets or back to Zeeland.

Roses that need a rootstock get grafted. "We perform bud grafting on the old-fashioned strong rootstock of *Rosa canina* 'Schmidt's Ideal'. The benefits are that the roses are healthier and have better resistance. There are also drawbacks: they

1. *ROSA* 'CHECKMATE'
2. *ROSA* 'LILAC WINE'

have suckers that you need to remove. They also last longer, which is a downside for us growers. Most rose growers use *Rosa corymbifera* 'Laxa' as the rootstock. Its success rate is higher, but after ten years it's exhausted. The *canina* we use can last for a hundred years, which is of course not relevant from a cultivation point of view. It also doesn't fit with the current gardening trends, where the idea is to turn your white garden into a purple garden after a few years. But well, we happen to prioritise healthy roses with good resistance. Although it would be more profitable if we went along with the hypes."

He believes a good relationship with his customers is more important than hypes. "They often say that they appreciate us making time for them. We're proud of that—that's what we want." He laughs. "But we can tell that some customers think, 'This is too much hassle, just give me the rose.'"

MANURE

In addition to roses, the nursery also sells tailor-made organic fertiliser. "It bothered me that everyone uses the same rose fertiliser, whether they are gardening in clay,

sand or peat," says Hans. "This way, you only fertilise the rose and not the soil. We developed rose fertiliser made up of nutrients and trace elements that are not only useful to the plant but also encourage the soil life. That's important, because rose roots work together with fungi and bacteria in the soil." For its customers, De Bierkreek has developed tailor-made mixtures designed for a particular type of rose, soil type and time of year. There is a Spring mix, Summer mix and an Autumn mix, for poor soil, sandy soil, peat soil, clay soil and standard soil. Customers who can't remember when their roses need to be fertilised can get a fertiliser subscription at De Bierkreek. For a fixed annual fee, they get sent the right amount of fertiliser for the right soil at the right time.

EXCEPTIONAL ROSES

How does De Bierkreek determine which roses are included in their product range and which not? "We do this by keeping an eye on which roses win prizes. Those roses have a certain quality; they have proved to be strong and healthy. My view is that us growers have a role to play in promoting them. If you attend the inspections like I do, you'll often be ahead of the curve because you see the roses before they go on sale. 'Let me know when they come on the market,' I'll tell the grower."

They get new rose varieties from large rose firms like Kordes and Tantau (in Germany). "But smaller breeders—like David Kenny (Ireland), Colin Dickson (Northern Ireland), Gareth Fryer and Chris Warner (England), Martin Vissers and Lens Roses (Belgium)—are also important. And let's not forget the amateur breeders like George MacPhail (Canada), Pierre Rutten (France), Sharlene Sutter (Switzerland) or Kim Rupert (US). These amateur breeders often come up with surprising varieties! Many smaller breeders have varieties that most people don't know about. If I promote them, I'll have interesting roses that the large breeding companies don't have. For example, not many people buy *Rosa* 'Checkmate'. And why does no one have the incredibly beautiful 'Lilac Wine'? I have a market for precisely these kinds of roses. It can take a few years before such a rose gets more publicity. But I have a climbing rose from Ton ter Linden, for example, that he discovered himself. We've been growing it and, after a slow start, this rose is now doing really well."

INSECTS

De Bierkreek has a striking number of roses that are attractive to insects. "People call them bee plants," says Hans, "but I'd rather call them insect plants. Pollen is an important food source not only for wild bees but also for adult hoverflies, lacewings and parasitic wasps. The larvae of these species are the main enemies of aphids and other pests. Bee plants are a hype. You hear everyone say that a rose with an open flower is a bee plant, but that's not true. Some of the open roses are attractive to bees, but others aren't. And there are insects that also squeeze into full blooms. If you really want to do something with roses, you're best off with native, indigenous roses. They are much better than any other rose shrub. We've got eight or nine varieties in that category."

3.

1. *ROSA* 'DOLCE'
2. *ROSA* 'EVELINE WILD'
3. *ROSA* 'NADIA ZEROUALI'

Edible roses

None of De Bierkreek's roses have been sprayed with pesticides and they are all therefore edible. They are certainly very healthy, but not always that tasty. That's why the breeding company Pheno Geno developed a series of roses that are truly delicious. The pink petals of both 'Dolce' and 'Renée van Wegberg' are sweet and fruity, and taste like raspberries. 'Eveline Wild', named after a famous Austrian TV chef, has apricot-coloured flowers that taste sweet. The yellow flowers of 'Nadia Zerouali', named after a Dutch culinary author, remind you of citrus and lemongrass. The pink flowers of 'Pear' could only taste of one thing, which is of course pears. And anyone who loves strawberries will enjoy 'Theo Clevers'. Theo Clevers is a master ice-cream maker who uses rose petals in his ice cream. "Edible roses are a lot of fun, and delicious," says Hans. "They are doing really well—demand outstrips the supply. We also get orders from food forests, but the conditions there are far too rough; the roses would never survive. Edible roses are shrub roses for in the garden and they need fertiliser."

FAVOURITES

When Hans is asked what his favourite roses are, he immediately lists a whole bunch. Starting with the insect plant 'Abigail Adams', a rose that's not easy to get your hands on. But it turns out to not be so bad after all: "We're due to get 123 of them," says Hans. "Another favourite of mine is the shrub rose 'Esvelda Newton', which you can also get to climb a wall. 'Fujisanensis' comes from Japan and has small hips that are clustered together in clouds. I also really love Ted Verschuren's Waterfall roses such as 'Amalia Falls', 'Angel Falls', 'Niagara Falls', 'Tugela Falls', 'Utigord Falls' and 'Yosemite Falls'. Waterfall roses. It's incredible what these ramblers bring to the table in terms of growth, beauty and autumn colours. On top of that, insects love them. 'Miss Kate' is one of the healthiest roses we know, and very popular with insects. Some other beautiful roses are 'Apple Jack', 'Charming', 'Lullaby' and 'Newsflash', all from the Irish rose grower David Kenny.

THE ROSE NURSERY DE BIERKREEK
Zevenhofstedenstraat 9, 4515 RK Biervliet (Zeeland), Netherlands
Opening hours Friday afternoon from 13:00 to 17:00 and Saturday from 08:30 to 17:00. The roses are also for sale online all year round.
www.bierkreek.nl
(For sales outlets elsewhere in the Netherlands and Belgium)

THE JOY OF
roses

THE PLANT
BREEDER

The plant breeder

Roses can be propagated in various ways

Roses can be propagated in various ways. One of the ways in which this can be done is bud grafting (also known as T-budding), a simple form of grafting. Basically you combine a wild, strong rose with a rose you want to propagate, with the intention of making it into a single plant.

BUD GRAFTING

The bud grafting method is often used because it has a lot of benefits, one of which is that it's easier than other kinds of grafting and therefore doesn't take as long. A practised bud grafter can set between a hundred and two hundred buds (eyes) per hour. They then let someone else do the binding. A nice plus of T-budding is that the success rate is often higher than in other forms of grafting. Also, the wounds are smaller.

The bud grafter works in July and August, when the bark of the wild rootstock comes loose easily. With a sharp grafting knife, a T-shaped incision is made in the bark of the wild rootstock, which is then folded out on both sides. The grafter then cuts off a piece of bark that has a well-developed bud (eye) from the rose they want to propagate. That eye is placed in the T-shaped cut that was just made in the wild rootstock. The bud is then bound on. In the spring, the wild rose is cut off diagonally just above the new, young shoot. What remains is a wild stem from which a cultivated rose grows. The wild rose has vigorous growth, so this will benefit the cultivar attached to it.

 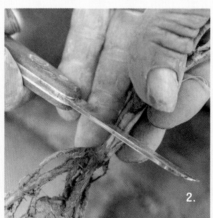 

1. THE PIECE OF BARK WITH THE EYE
   IS PLACED IN THE T-SHAPED INCISION
2. CUTTING OF BARK
3. TIE OFF WITH A 'FLEISCHHAUER'

Stock

The dog rose (*Rosa canina*) was usually used in the past as the rootstock. It still gets used today, but new rootstock options have come on the market over the course of time. Nowadays, most growers use *Rosa corymbifera* 'Laxa' as the rootstock. Its success rate is almost ninety per cent and you don't get any suckers. The disadvantage is that this rootstock only lasts ten years.

Raffia or rubber?

In the past, the T-budded rose was bound with raffia. The raffia rotted away eventually, so the thickening rootstock did not get constricted. Right after the Second World War, raffia was scarce and thin rubber strips entered the market from Denmark. In the early 1950s they were replaced by a German product, the Fleischhauer OSV (Okulations-Schnellverschluss), a wide rubber strip with a staple through it. It's much more expensive than raffia, but is less work.

4.

"GETTING A BEAUTIFUL FLOWER IS THE EASIEST THING THERE IS. BUT FOR ME IT'S ABOUT THE ENTIRE SHRUB"

Martin Vissers

BREEDER OF NO-NONSENSE ROSES

If you accompany a rose breeder walking through his rose fields, it's best not to say anything. As soon as I call out, "Oh, what a beautiful rose!" I get corrected: "No, it's too tall. I'm getting rid of that one." A bit further along I see one I could quite happily take home with me, but: "It doesn't have any leaves at the bottom: it's diseased. And that one over there, with the brown buds... That one has to go too, no matter how beautiful the flower is."

These fields aren't called 'trial fields' for nothing. They are where the Belgian rose breeder Martin Vissers tries out his roses. Where I see one wonderful rose after another, he mainly sees defects. "If you walk here in June, you think: what beautiful roses," he says. "But what I'm mainly thinking is: ditch it, ditch it, ditch it. Getting a beautiful flower is the easiest thing there is, but for me it's about the entire shrub. It has got to have quality and character and offer something new.'

Martin Vissers is one of the most famous rose breeders in the world. That's why it's all the more surprising that he wanted nothing to do with roses until well into middle age. He loved gardening, and had planted and sown all sorts of things in his garden. "Even those difficult blue poppies did well in my garden. But roses? Nope... no roses! I didn't want them,

thought they were too difficult, too complex. The pruning and those eyes and the diseases, and this and that and so on and so forth."

When he was thirty, Martin started a thriving business in adhesive and sealant products, which he decided to sell after twenty years. It was in 1998 and he was fifty. "And then I got interested in roses. It was a combination of circumstances. The sale of my business meant I had time on my hands. I met the rose breeder Jef Orye and on his advice I became a member of Rosica, the Flemish amateur club of rose breeders. It was the best time of my life, as I was able to concentrate fully on breeding roses. But the deciding factor was a book I read about the legendary rose breeder Louis Lens. When I finished it I thought, 'I want to continue his work!' An extra stimulus was that after his death in 2001, a large part of his archive was entrusted to me."

Martin did a course in genetics and founded the rose breeding company Viva International. "The first year I made crossings myself, I had 127 seedlings. They produced eight top-class roses, including 'Midsummersnow', 'Peter Paul Rubens', 'Sweet Blondie' and 'Taxandria'. That's beginner's luck; I'll never be able to replicate it." Because he hadn't forgotten how difficult he used to think roses were, he

1. POLLEN IS COLLECTED (PHOTO TAKEN AT DE RUITER INNOVATIONS)
2. DISH WITH POLLEN (PHOTO TAKEN AT DE RUITER INNOVATIONS)

decided to dedicate himself to breeding roses that are so strong and healthy that they need very little care. He called them "no-nonsense roses". "I try to select roses that also do well with people who don't have green fingers. Roses that don't just have beautiful flowers, but where the shrub itself is also beautiful. Roses that bloom for a long time with flowers that smell nice. Healthy roses that are disease-resistant. Because nowadays no one wants to spray anymore, right?"

He doesn't do it so the world can have even more roses than the tens of thousands of cultivars that already exist. "There are plenty of roses, but not enough good roses. I want to improve and add to what's already there." And that's exactly what he does. Many of the roses he develops are so spectacular that they win one award after another at rose competitions.

CROSSING

What does a breeder do exactly? "To cross roses, you need parent plants. You start by castrating the rose: removing everything male. Whenever I give a talk somewhere and I get to this point, I always recommend that the male members of the audience cover their ears for a while... From May to August, I apply pollen from the father plant to the carpel of the mother plant. I do that with my finger, which I lick clean

every time. Maybe there's something in the saliva that's good for fertilisation, because I have a lot of success with the seeds sprouting. I mainly work indoors, otherwise you get helpers in the form of bees. Once the roses have been pollinated, they get a label saying which is the father and which is the mother."

A few months after the crossing, the mother plants grow rose hips full of seeds. "Those hips are refrigerated for three months to simulate the winter period. In December, I pick out the seeds. I clean them and sow them in trays with special soil and a layer of Rhine sand over the top to keep them moist. And I add a label and I make sure no mice get at them. The first seedlings might appear after three weeks, but it can also take two years. The seedlings are potted and then planted in the trial field. No selections are made in the first year. They need to be given time to build disease resistance. But after that it's merciless: if it's diseased, has lousy blooms, can't cope with rain or sun, doesn't flower a lot, weak growth... out it goes! They don't receive any care, except for starter fertilisation. If they do well here in the sandy Kempen soil, they'll do well anywhere. That's what a trial field is for, right?"

Seeing a new rose blooming for the first time is like unwrapping a Christmas present, he says. "I T-bud three to five examples of what I feel are the better varieties.

ROSA 'ESPRIT D'AMOUR'

I make a small trial planting of the selected roses from these varieties. After I've taken another selection from them, larger trial plantings follow. I enter the best of those roses in international rose competitions, where they are monitored for two to three years and evaluated by professionals and an international jury. That's essentially the final selection. Based on those results, I decide which roses I want to continue with. I apply for plant breeder's rights and the rose is then T-budded or propagated using cuttings by professional breeders. It takes ten years before you're sure whether you've managed it, and another ten to market the rose. Yes, you need a lot of patience." Does he have that patience? "No. Except with roses."

Martin's speciality is *paniculata* roses, which have thousands of single flowers in a dense cluster on each stem. They look like panicled hydrangeas, but they flower for longer. The panicles can reach 50cm or more and they attract an exceptional number of bees and other pollinators. "*Paniculatas* are my trademark," says Martin. "I have them in different growth categories: shrubs, clusters, climbing and even ramblers. Well, I like doing crazy things: I see it as a challenge. My first real *paniculata* was 'Esprit d'Amour', which is usually available as a rose grown from its own roots. They are used as border plants, shrubs or climbing roses."

THE FUTURE

How does he see the future of the rose? "When I look at the future, I expect to see many roses in public parks that have been cultivated from cuttings—from their own roots, in other words. They don't need much care, are climate-proof, live for a long time and don't develop suckers. If you plant shrub roses and groundcover roses, no weeds can get through. Potted roses also have a promising future. With the increasing shortage of building land, gardens are becoming smaller and smaller, and many garden lovers end up in apartments. That's why I've been working a lot with potted roses and miniature roses for the past few years."

And what is his opinion on edible roses? "That's a small niche market, not a market you can make a living from. Rose petals and rose hips have been used for centuries in liqueurs, pastries and even medicines. All very nice, but to breed roses specifically for that purpose... no. For me it's about roses in the garden."

For the large rose firms, he says, cut roses are the most important commodity. "Garden roses make up only 5 to 15 per cent of the business; the rest is cut roses. They are selected for vase life rather than for their fragrance. There are two reasons why cut rose nurseries are located around the equator: it's cheap, and you're allowed to spray pesticides. That's why there are lakes in Africa that are dead —not a single fish remains in them. But that's changing, fortunately."

FAVOURITES

Well, and then we get to the banal but unavoidable question of which roses are his favourites. "The shrub and climbing rose 'Amourin' is my favourite. 'Esprit d'Amour' as well. Both are wonderfully aromatic. But my best rose is probably 'Midsummersnow', a no-nonsense white rose. The prettiest paniculata is 'Argus' and of the groundcover roses I'd choose 'Green Summer'; weeds don't stand a chance with that one. 'Palsy Walsy', my most acclaimed rose, has a special place in my heart. My best-selling rose is 'Minerva'. A hundred thousand plants of that cluster rose variety are sold every year. And then there's the *persica* hybrid 'Persian Sun' and the *persica* climber 'Persian Dawn'. One beautiful rambler is 'Skyblizzard'. And 'New Dreams' is a shrub rose, but also works as a climber. As you see, roses are extremely versatile."

"WHAT COMES OUT OF A BUD IS A SURPRISE EVERY TIME"

Hans de Ruiter and Ad van Rooijen

BREEDERS OF CUT ROSES AND POTTED ROSES

You can't be too soft-hearted when going into a greenhouse with two rose breeders. While they are calmly explaining how plant breeding works, their watchful eyes see everything going on around them. When they approach a tray with about twenty different-coloured seedlings they first say lovingly, "Look, these are all brothers and sisters." And then they pull five of those sisters and brothers out of the soil: "Not good enough."

And when you've only just recovered from the shock, you come across an employee whose entire job is decapitating roses. Beautiful red, white and pink flowers all end up in a large bio-container. They have to go, because flowers suck the energy out of a plant. And it badly needs that energy to make nice rose hips full of seeds that will later be used to create new roses.

Being a breeder... it seems like a cruel profession. But whether you believe it or not, breeders love their roses. "What comes out of a bud is a surprise every time," says Hans de Ruiter. As the son and grandson of rose breeders, he is the third generation in this company. "From the age of seven I was helping out, for twenty-five cents an hour."

THE 'ROSES OF TOMORROW'

We are at De Ruiter Innovations in Amstelveen, a breeding and propagation company for cut roses (60 per cent of its business) and potted roses (30 per cent). The remaining 10 per cent are rose-hip, cluster, garden and patio roses. Here, Hans de Ruiter and Ad van Rooijen develop new roses. Or, as they call them, the 'roses of tomorrow'. In greenhouses covering a total of about 7000m², they breed and select the greenhouse roses and potted roses. By 'potted roses' they mean small roses that are cultivated in the greenhouse and are bought by consumers to be kept indoors on their tables or windowsills.

1. THE HIPS OF *ROSA* 'HIPHOP' ARE GROWN FOR CUTTING
2. CUTTING ROSE 'TRIVIA'
3. GARDEN ROSE 'WHITE VALEDA'
4. REMOVING REJECTED SEEDLINGS FROM POTTED ROSES
5. POTTED ROSES

1. *ROSA* 'PERFUMED BUBBLES' IS A CUT ROSE WITH
   MULTIPLE FLOWERS ON THE SAME STEM
2. GREENHOUSE WITH ROSES FOR CUTTING
3. BLOOMING ROOM

CUT ROSES

"There are lots of things you need to pay attention to when breeding cut roses," says Ad. "First of all, the health of the plant. And then everything that makes it economically viable: you want cut roses to have a long shelf life and to be easy to transport. We also take account of consumers' wishes, because they keep changing. Popular colours today are brown and terra; The brownish-pink flowers of our new *Rosa* 'Moccachino' fit in with that trend. And we're working on a black cluster rose. Another fashion factor is the shape of the rose. Currently, the favourite flower shape is more quartered. We're also working on the fragrance, but creating a scent line is pretty difficult. It doesn't provide any added value either, as shelf life is the most important thing for cut roses."

After the selection, the seedlings are sent to a country where they're expected to do well. "Every year, 7,000 of our roses go to Kenya and 4,000 go to Ecuador, where they are developed further. Many of the roses are then exported from Kenya to Europe, and from Ecuador to North America. It's too expensive to grow cut roses in the Netherlands. The labour costs are higher and the greenhouses consume energy." He laughs. "Around the equator the sun is free."

DNA

De Ruiter Innovations uses traditional breeding and selection methods, but they also deploy modern techniques. "If you cross a greenhouse rose," Ad explains, "it takes five or six years before you know what properties the new rose has. We look at the roses' DNA so that we can later identify certain properties. It's a toolbox, letting us work faster and more efficiently. This way, we can also detect certain diseases and pests. In the lab, we try to give the roses a disease and if there's a rose that doesn't get sick, it is resistant. Then we look at the DNA: is there a difference between the group that's sick and the group that isn't sick? We flag that difference in the DNA—this is called a marker. We use markers to analyse the properties of the roses." But even then, the rose must always still be tested. "For a cut rose, that takes six years; for a garden rose, it's ten to twelve. That's because of climate influences. And disease pathogens also mutate; that's why we have to cross to stay on top of the diseases."

Now that more and more chemical agents are getting banned, the susceptibility of roses to harmful insects is also being taken into consideration. "We don't spray our roses growing outdoors, not even for aphids," says Hans. "We hang up cards with the eggs of parasitic wasps. Indoors, we spray with organic agents that increase the resilience of the rose. Products such as neem oil make the plant less attractive for insects. In the past, we would spray and that would kill off all the insects. Now, we want to keep the beneficial insects, like parasitic wasps."

BLOOMING ROOM

In the blooming room, tests are conducted to see how long cut roses stay attractive in a vase. The temperature is 20°C, the light is normal. "The cut roses have been travelling by ship for forty days," says Ad. "Transport by ship is cheaper than by plane and the carbon footprint is more sustainable. They are immobilised and transported at 1°C. We put them in a vase, check what they look like and see how many days they look good for." The shelf life of the potted roses is also tested here. "They stand in our test room for at least three weeks, during which time they shouldn't discolour too much. Not many make it, and the rejects get thrown out. Well, we have to do that. People pay good money for them."

DE RUITER INNOVATIONS B.V.
Meerlandenweg 55, 1187 ZR Amstelveen, Netherlands.
www.deruiter.com

THE JOY OF

roses

ROSES
IN THE GARDEN

Roses in the garden

Roses thrive in any type of soil as long as you add what they need to it

Roses have few requirements for the soil they are in. They just don't appreciate acidic soil as much. They can also struggle in places that are very wet or very dry, so it's better not to plant them there.

THE SOIL AND THE PLANTS

Roses grow best in fertile, well-drained soil. Loam soil and light clay are ideal, but they also do well in sand and heavy clay. Heavy clay is fertile and retains water well, but in the summer, when it's warm and dry for long periods, the soil becomes a hard and impenetrable crust. You can loosen the soil by mixing the clay with compost and/or sand.

Sandy soil heats up quickly, but doesn't retain moisture and nutrients as well. This can be improved by adding organic material to it such as compost, clay minerals or sandy soil improvers (bentonite).

Planting potted roses in the garden

Roses that were grown in a pot are sold all year round. You can plant them out all year round, except when it's freezing. Dig a hole that's twice as deep and wide as the pot. Dip the rose including the pot in a bucket of water, remove the rose from the pot and put it in the hole. Fill in the space around the clump of roots with the soil you just dug up. Make sure that the bud union (the thickening between the roots and the branches) is 3-5cm underground. Press the soil down firmly. Make a mini-trench around the plant so the water does not drain away. Water the plant slowly with a bucket of water. Cover the soil around the rose with a mulch layer of fallen leaves, compost or straw to prevent evaporation. During the first few months, check regularly whether the rose needs water.

Acidic soil

If you live in an area with acidic soil and still want roses in your garden, it's possible as long as you take a few extra measures. Fill the plant hole with a generous quantity of compost. Give the plants blood meal and bone meal in the spring. In the autumn, add well-digested or dried farmyard manure around the base of the plant. And sprinkle some lime around the roses every winter.

Roses for poor sandy soil

— 'Alchymist'
— 'Ballerina'
   (hybrid moschata or
   hybrid musk)
— 'Betty Prior'
— 'Fru Dagmar Hastrup'
— 'Ghislaine de Féligonde'
— 'Guirlande d'Amour',
   also sold as 'Lenalbi'
— 'Kew Gardens'
— 'Roseraie de l'Hay'
— *Rosa* x *centifolia* 'Major',
   also known as
   'Rose des Peintres'
— *Rosa rugosa*

1.   *ROSA* 'BALLERINA'
2.   *ROSA* 'BETTY PRIOR'

Planting roses with bare roots

Roses are also sold without a pot and without potting compost, so you can see the roots. They are available from November to March and are appropriately called 'bare-root roses'. These roses should also not be planted when it's freezing. They do need to be planted as soon as possible, or the roots will dry out. You don't have to leave them in a bucket of water for a day or a night, despite what gardening books and the Internet say. If you leave the roots in a bucket of water for half an hour before planting, they will have enough moisture. Cut off damaged roots and shorten each thick tap root by a third. This encourages the thinner lateral roots to grow.

Dig a hole 60cm deep and 30cm wide and loosen the subsoil thoroughly. Put a mixture of garden soil and potting compost at the bottom but don't sprinkle any fertiliser in the plant hole. Lower the rose into the hole. Make sure that the bud union is 3-5cm under the surface. Distribute the excavated soil evenly between the roots and shake the rose until the soil fits tightly around it. Press the soil around the plant down and give the plant a bucket of water. You can cover the soil around the rose with a mulch layer to prevent evaporation. During the first few months, check regularly whether the rose needs water.

DETERMINE THE PLANTING HOLE DEPTH: TOP OF POT MUST BE THE SAME AS THE GROUND LEVEL

GROUNDING A NEWLY PLANTED ROSE FOR THE WINTER

MULCHING WITH STRAW

ROSES WITH BARE ROOTS IN A BUCKET OF WATER

ADD ROSE SOIL

PRESS SOIL IN

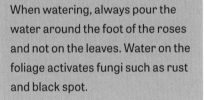

When watering, always pour the water around the foot of the roses and not on the leaves. Water on the foliage activates fungi such as rust and black spot.

Planting a climbing rose or rambler

Before you plant a climbing rose, you must make sure that there is a sturdy support it can grow up (see page 136). Dig a hole, loosen the soil in the hole, put the rose in it and fill the hole with soil. Make sure that the bud union is 3-5cm under the surface. Water the rose and add a mulch layer around it. After planting, leave the strongest branches and prune the weakest shoots to the ground.

A rambler that you want to grow up a tree should be planted 1m away from the trunk. If you put it any closer to the tree, the tree will absorb most of the water. Guide the rose towards the tree with a thick cord.

THE PLACE

Sunlight

The best place for roses is where they get 4-5 hours of sun a day. Less is OK, but then they won't grow as fast. If you have a garden with a lot of shade, put the roses somewhere where they at least get the morning sun.

Shade

There are roses that are happy in the semi-shade (meaning least four hours of sun per day in the summer). Examples are the alba hybrids 'Félicité Parmentier' and 'Madame Plantier', the rugosa rose 'Blanc Double de Coubert', the hybrid

Nematodes

Don't plant roses in soil that has had roses before, as that soil will contain nematodes that suck on the roots of roses. You can purge the soil by sowing marigolds in May. If you dig them into the soil in the autumn, the soil is decontaminated and suitable for planting roses in again. If you don't have anywhere for your new roses than where roses have already been, dig a large plant hole, fill a deep cardboard box with soil and plant the roses in there. By the time the cardboard has decomposed, the new roses will be strong enough to resist any nematodes.

Healthy soil has soil fungi that live in harmony with the plant roots. This lets the roots absorb water and food more easily. If the roots of the new roses receive ready-to-use mycorrhiza (soil fungi) during planting, the roses will grow so well that nematodes won't bother them.

1. RAMBLING ROSE IN A TREE
2. *ROSA* 'VEILCHENBLAU'

Bud union

The bud union must be 3-5cm under the surface because this will protect it better against drying out and frost. It also prevents the rootstock from sprouting and forming suckers. If that happens, some of the nutrients will go to the suckers rather than your rose.

Land of plenty

If you give the rose nutrients in the hole you plant it in, the roots will remain in that tasty land of plenty. So don't do that! Encourage the roots to go and find nutrients themselves by loosening the soil in the plant hole. This lets the roots penetrate the soil easily later on.

moschatas 'Ballerina', 'Bouquet Parfait' and 'Neige d'Été', the cluster rose 'Ville de Roeulx', the bush roses 'Gertrude Jekyll' and 'Lady of Shalott' and the climbing roses 'Pink Cloud', 'Buff Beauty' and 'Veilchenblau'.

Roses that can grow under trees with a lot of shade (no more than two hours of sun) include 'Zéphirine Drouhin' and ramblers. The field rose (*Rosa arvensis*) grows in the shade, but only flowers properly when it gets plenty of sun.

Space

Roses need a lot of space. That's why you shouldn't plant them too close to trees and shrubs. Don't plant your rose too close to a hedge either, especially if it's conifers, because hedges absorb a lot of water from the soil. If there is plenty of space between a rose and its neighbours this also allows the wind to reach it, so after a downpour the wet leaves get blown dry. But don't plant the rose where it gets a lot of wind as it doesn't like that.

The distance between roses should be the same as the height they'll eventually reach. For miniature roses that's 25cm, for grandiflora roses (hybrid tea) and cluster roses it's 35-40cm (i.e. five plants per m²), for groundcover roses of 50-60cm (three plants per m²), for hybrid moschatas of 50-100cm, for shrub roses 80-100cm, and 1.5-2m for climbing roses—or even more if they are ramblers.

HEDGES

You might never have considered enclosing all or part of your garden with a hedge of roses. Most people just choose the easiest way of demarcating the boundaries of the garden, namely a fence. But try to imagine a hedge of roses around the edge of your garden, rather than a fence. Or a conifer hedge with roses growing through it. Doesn't that sound wonderful?

Roses do great in a hedge. If you have enough space, you can plant one consisting of just roses. Many rose varieties are suitable for this. If you use wild roses, you get a dense, impenetrable hedge and a guarantee that you will not to be troubled by neighbourhood cats and dogs anymore. Moreover, you'll be doing many creatures a favour with a hedge like this. Butterflies, bees, hoverflies and parasitic wasps will come looking for pollen, and birds will use it as a shelter and feed on rose hips in the winter.

A rose hedge can be as low or as tall as you like. It can be a formal edge that doesn't get taller than 20cm, or a dense screen of 1.5 to 2m. If you don't have a lot of space, choose rose shrubs that grow straight upwards. If you want a wide hedge, plant two rows with roses alternating.

In addition to wild roses such as wrinkled roses (*Rosa rugosa*), dog roses (*Rosa canina*) or red-leaved roses (*Rosa glauca*), you can also make a hedge from rose bushes or low ramblers. If you want it to be nice and dense, plant the roses 40cm apart. You'll barely have to do any maintenance. Just like any other hedge, you can cut the roses into shape every now and then—but certainly not too often—with an (electric) hedge trimmer. After doing that, sprinkle a blended organic (rose) fertiliser at the base of the roses.

Very low hedge

The hybrid moschata 'Claire Jolly' doesn't get taller than 50cm.

Low hedge (50-100cm)

A wild rose suitable for a low hedge is *Rosa nitada* (50cm). Or you could us the patio rose 'Riverdance'. Roses that bloom for a long time are 'Ballerina' (50-100cm), 'Lavender Dream' (60-80cm) and Pavement roses from the City·flor product range (which can cope with poor soil, disease, salt and drought).

Medium-high hedge (1.0-1.5m)

A 1.5m hedge needs to be as wide as it is tall. That's definitely something to keep in mind from the start.

Wild roses that are suitable for a medium-high hedge are the sweetbriar rose *Rosa rubiginosa* (80-125cm, also nice in a loose, mixed hedge with hawthorn and green privet) and *Rosa rugosa* (1.0-1.5m).

A rose that blooms for a long time is 'F.J. Grootendorst' (1.0-1.20m).

A rose that gets a lot of rose hips is 'Fru Dagmar Hastrup' (1m).

The repeat-flowering shrub rose 'Rose de Rescht' is a historic rose with compact growth. Finally, two more hybrid moschatas: 'Neige d'Été (1.2cm-1.5m) and 'Rush' (1.5m).

Tall hedge

Many wild roses grow fast and can easily become 1.5-2m tall and wide. They only flower once, and do so for about four weeks. Some hybrid moschatas are also suitable for a tall hedge. They don't grow as fast as wild roses and bloom from June to October.

Examples of wild roses

— Dog rose *Rosa canina* (2m)
— *Rosa moyesii* (up to 3m)
— *Rosa moyesii* 'Nevada' (2m)

Other roses suitable for a hedge

— 'Bukavu' (1.0-1.5m, grows straight upwards)
— 'Cornelia' (1.5-1.7m, can handle shade)
— 'Climbing Iceberg' (4m)
— 'Duchesse de Montebello' (1.5-1.8m, few thorns)
— 'Elmshorn' (1.2-1.5m)
— 'Maria Mathilda' (70-100cm)
— 'Mozart' (1.2-1.5m)
— 'Pink Magic' (up to 1.5m)
— 'Port Sunlight' (1.0-1.4m)
— 'Robusta' (1.5-2.0m)
— 'Sally Holmes' (1.2-1.5m)
— 'Souvenir de Louis Lens' (1.7-2.0m)
— 'The Lark Ascending' (1.2-1.5m)
— 'White Magic' (up to 1.5m)
— 'Wisley 2008' (1.2-1.5m)

1. *ROSA* 'LAVENDER DREAM'
   (60-80CM)
2. *ROSA RUGOSA* 'RUBRA'
   (1,5-2M)
3. *ROSA RUGOSA*
   'PINK GROOTENDORST' (1M)
4. *ROSA* 'FRU DAGMAR HASTRUP'
   (1M)
5. *ROSA* 'BUKAVU' (1-1,5M)
6. *ROSA* 'MOZART' (1,2-1,5M)
7. *ROSA* 'ELMSHORN' (1,2-1,5M)

BALCONY AND PATIO

The word 'rose' might make you think of a garden with rose shrubs in all possible colours and pergolas overgrown with climbing roses. But why couldn't the roses be in a pot? Especially now that newly-built homes tend to come with smaller gardens and more and more people are living in apartments, either by choice or from necessity.

You could squeeze a garden rose into a pot and say it's a rose for on the patio or balcony, but no dedicated rose breeder would be satisfied with that solution. They prefer to get to work on developing roses that remain small and compact, which they call 'patio roses'. These roses look like cluster roses, with their clusters full of flowers, but they're much smaller.

Then the breeders thought: while we're at it we might as well make roses that are even smaller and can cope with being in a pot on the windowsill or the dining table. That's why for a while now the market has been flooded with miniature roses, mini roses, baby roses, dwarf roses and whatever else all those teeny-tiny roses get called. Small roses don't have deep roots, so they're content with a 30x30cm home.

Are there roses that are absolutely not suitable for growing in pots? "Definitely," says Steven van Dalen from rose nursery De Wilde. "Old rose varieties aren't a good choice for a pot because they only bloom for a short time. You'll be looking at a green shrub for most of the summer. I wouldn't put a rambler in a pot either. A pot needs a rose that is decorative, bushy, with a lot of full flowers that keep on blooming."

Miniature roses

Miniature roses don't get taller than 40cm, have lots of small flowers in clusters and usually don't have a scent. Miniature climbing roses are repeat-flowering climbing roses with small leaves and flowers. Some are fragrant.

Mini or dwarf roses are called that because they stay small. But given that some can grow to 40cm, you may wonder what the difference is between a dwarf rose and a miniature rose.

What pot?

The roots of a rose grow vertically rather than laterally. When they reach the bottom of the pot, the rose stops growing. The larger the pot, the happier the rose feels. If you buy a rose in a pot with the intention of putting it on your patio or balcony, put it in a pot that's at least one and a half times larger when you get at home. It needs to be at least 45cm deep and wide. For climbing roses, it's better to take one that's at least 60cm wide and 50cm high. This gives the roots enough space and the shrub won't dry out as fast. Once a rose has matured, give it a pot that's as tall as it is. Choose a pot with enough drainage holes to allow excess water to drain away.

VASILI TROPININ
GIRL WITH ROSES (1850)

Preventing overheating

The roots of roses must not get overheated. That's why you shouldn't put the rose in a dark-coloured pot. Dark pots absorb heat, whereas lighter-coloured pots reflect heat.

Terracotta

Plant the roses in a terracotta pot. Moisture can evaporate more quickly from these pots. Check that there are one or more drainage holes at the bottom of the pot so that the excess rainwater can drain away. If the roots are in water for a long time, the rose will grow poorly or die. Stand the pot on stones or legs so that the excess water can drain away easily.

Planting

If the potted rose is to be kept outdoors all winter, you should take this into account when planting it. You do that by covering the inside of the pot with jute or with a protective lining made of sheep's wool. Don't cover the drainage holes at the bottom, so water can drain away. Put a layer of pot shards, gravel or clay pellets at the bottom for the drainage. Fill one third of the pot with potting soil or rose soil, enriched with compost. Dip the roots of the rose in a bucket of water for a few minutes. Then put it in the pot, hold it with one hand and fill the pot with potting compost or rose soil. Make sure the bud union (the nodule on the thick stem that the branches grow from) is 3-5cm below the soil surface. Water the plant and put it in a place where it gets four to six hours of sunlight every day. It's best if the plant is in the sun and the pot in the shade, so the pot doesn't get overheated.

Care

Potted roses can't cope with the soil drying out; the clump around the roots must always be a little bit moist. In addition to water, they also need nutrients. Give them rose fertiliser or put a slow-release fertiliser tablet in the potting soil every year. Alternatively, mix liquid nutrition for patio plants into the watering water every three weeks between March and August. Dead-head faded blooms. Prune the rose back in early spring and treat the plant with rose fertiliser afterwards.

Replace the top layer of the potting compost with fresh soil each autumn. Repot larger roses into a larger pot with fresh potting compost every three years.

Put potted roses that are kept indoors in a bright spot where there is no draught. Don't put them above a radiator. Water regularly and make sure the excess water can drain away.

1. PLACE POT SHARDS IN THE BOTTOM OF THE POT
2. FILL THE POT WITH ROSE SOIL
3. PLANT THE ROSE IN THE POT
4. ADD A HANDFUL OF ROSE FERTILISER
5. DEAD-HEAD FLOWERS THAT HAVE FADED

Roses for small pots

For small pots (at least 30x30cm), the obvious choice is
a patio rose or miniature rose. These roses are grown
specifically for pots. Their roots aren't as deep and they stay
small. Good options are:
— 'Bijenweelde' (60cm)
— 'Crystal Fairy' (50cm)
— 'Flirt 2011' (50-70cm)
— 'Raspberry Royale' (40cm)
— 'Sweet Dream' (60cm)
— 'Zwergenfee' (30-40cm)

Roses for medium-sized pots

Groundcover roses and smaller climbing roses grown for
patios are larger than miniature roses, but still small enough
to put in a pot (at least 45x45cm). Choose for example:
— 'Christopher Marlowe'
— 'Flower Carpet Coral'
— 'Little White Pet'
— 'Mariatheresia'
— 'Pink Blanket'

Roses for large pots

Shrub, climbing and rambling roses grow vigorously
and need a pot of at least 60x60cm. Examples of vigorous
growers:
— 'Kew Gardens'
— 'Lady of Shalott'
— 'Open Arms'
— 'Princess Anne'
— 'Strawberry Hill'

Some more examples of patio and miniature roses

— 'Baby Love'
— 'Bluesette'
— 'Little Pim'
— 'Palsy Walsy'
— 'Para Ti'
— 'Pink Blanket'
— 'Poppy Rose'
— 'Stadt Rom'
— 'Starlet Melina'
— 'Sun Hit'

Fragrant roses for pots

— 'Amber Queen' (80-100cm)
— 'Bonica' (60-80cm)
— 'Friesia' (60-80cm)
— 'Queen Mother' (50-60cm)
— 'Ruby Anniversary' (40-60cm)
— 'Schneewittchen' (60-80cm)
— 'Shine On' (30-50cm)

1. *ROSA* 'PINK BLANKET'
2. *ROSA* 'LADY OF SHALOTT'
3. *ROSA* 'STADT ROM'
4. *ROSA* 'BIJENWEELDE'

"THERE'S A SECTION WITH DARK RED, PURPLE AND DABS OF LIGHT BLUE THAT REGULARLY MOVES VISITORS TO TEARS"

Martje van den Bosch

**OWNER OF DE TUINEN IN DEMEN,
COLOUR SPECIALIST**

Martje van den Bosch's garden was created in a number of stages. She started in 1989, when she and her husband Fridtjof moved to an old, dilapidated house in the village of Demen. It had a small front garden and back garden. In their spare time, Fridtjof renovated the house, and Martje played around in the garden. "I didn't have a lot of experience with gardening," she says. "You can tell from the colours of the flowers I planted back then. They are sensible colours, colours you can't go wrong with. It would be boring if that was the end of it."

But it wasn't. In 2003, Martje and Fridtjof bought the neighbour's land. The pigsty that was there was demolished and a large greenhouse was built on the vacated land. The more time Martje spent gardening, the more fun she had. But she found she needed more and more space for all her ideas and the associated plants. "Fortunately, the meadow a little further along became available, and we bought that too. From that point on, it became a whole different story. I had started looking into colour combinations with plants and experimenting with combining saturated reds, deep purples and ice blues." The garden, which is now 1.5 hectares in size, is divided into sixteen sections separated by beech hedges. They are planted with different groups of colour. "I

find the colours evoke something in visitors," says Martje. "For example, there's a section with dark red, purple and dabs of light blue that regularly moves visitors to tears. It's a combination of being touched by the colours and the person you are. Not everyone sheds a tear, but if they do, that's where. Whereas the orange rose garden makes most people happy, and they say the circular white garden inspires reflection."

That white garden is one of the showpieces. When you enter this section, you immediately feel it: there is peace here and harmony here. It's hard to pinpoint why exactly. The circular shape? The white roses? "You don't have to figure that out," says Martje, "as long as you feel at ease here." There are people who choose this spot to get married, she says. "But we've also had a funeral, with sixty white chairs and the coffin in the middle. It's no coincidence that people react so strongly to the colour white. White is about dignity, purity. That's why this colour seems to suit the ceremonial: you wouldn't do something like that in an orange garden."

Two other showstoppers are the arbours, one of which is covered with 88 climbing roses. They have colour gradients from white through soft pink to red and from white through soft yellow to orange-red. The same colours can be found in

1. *ROSA* 'FAITHFUL' WITH *PHLOX PANICULATA* 'VAN GOGH'
2. ROSE ARCADE
3. WHITE GARDEN
4. *ROSA* 'GISCARD D'ESTAING'

the borders next to them. "I start with the idea for the colour palette," Martje explains. "The colours in the borders have to match the colours of the arbour."

It is not just the colours that are striking, so are the contrasts.

And no, that's not a coincidence: "A rose has a circular or semi-circular shape, so you can add a red hot poker or a lupin as a contrast. You mustn't overdo it though. If you have too much contrast, it gets overwhelming. If you don't have enough, it becomes boring. It's a matter of looking carefully: what contrasts with what?" She doesn't have rules for combinations with roses. "Except that I consciously think about ensuring a balance." She shows what a beautiful combination the Turk's cap lily (*Lilium martagon*) makes with roses. And *Rosa* 'Purple Skyliner' with *Clematis*. "Geraniums also go well with roses because the way the geraniums grow hides and masks the stiff foliage of the roses. You do have to be careful, though, that the roses don't get smothered by the geraniums. Roses and delphiniums are another lovely combination, as are roses and lavender. But lavender doesn't like clay so it's not an option here. Salvias and catmint look similar to lavender and they work a lot better here. And for something exciting, I like combining roses with red hot pokers and phloxes. 'Life without phlox is a mistake,' said the famous grower Karl Förster. And he was right."

In the beginning, Martje attached a lot of importance to symmetry. "But I'm letting that go more and more. The rigidity of it is starting to annoy me. Moreover, you end up fighting a losing battle. If you plant two borders that mirror each other, you'll notice after a time that the plants grow fast on one side, but start dying on the other side. And that's the end of your symmetry. What's much more important is the rhythm."

One of her favourite roses is *Rosa* 'Westerland'. "This rose has everything you might want in a rose. It's a healthy climber with good foliage. The cup-shaped flowers are a bit floppy and have soft orange hues that blend into each other. It flowers all summer and attracts a lot of bees. As icing on the cake, 'Westerland' also has a scent that cheers you up."

Martje has written a book about what effect colour combinations can have on people. It is called *De beleving van kleur in de tuin* (How colour is experienced in the garden).

Climbers emulating standard roses

"The grafting point of a standard rose is high up, making it vulnerable," says Martje. "Instead of standard roses, we use climbing roses. Their grafting point is below ground level, making them less vulnerable. We prune such climbing roses so they are bare except at the top. This gives a rose that looks like a standard rose, but isn't."

1. ROSA 'FAIREST CAPE', TURK'S CAP LILY (*LILIUM MARTAGON* 'CLAUDE SHRIDE' AND 'ARABIAN NIGHT'), RED ORACHE (*ATRIPLEX HORTENSIS*), *HELENIUM* (NOT IN BLOOM), FENNEL (*FOENICULUM VULGARE* 'GIANT BRONZE')
2. ROSA 'PURPLE SKYLINER' WITH *CLEMATIS* 'JACKMANII'
3. ROSA 'FELLOWSHIP', KNIPHOFIA, DAY LILY (*HEMEROCALLIS*), GLADIOLI (*GLADIOLUS*)
4. ROSA 'GOLDEN GATE'

DE TUINEN IN DEMEN
Kleine Poelstraat 13, 5354 KD Demen, Netherlands.
Opening hours for the public: from 24 April to 4 September every Thursday and Sunday from 11:00 to 17:00. In June, an annual rose day is organized. More information can be found on the website.
www.detuinenindemen.nl

WHICH PLANTS COMBINE WELL WITH ROSES?

I read in a book about roses that a garden can be full of flowering plants, but something is really wrong if there are no roses among them. However, a garden with nothing but roses is rather boring. Try taking a walk around a rose garden without falling asleep. You can't. If you want a beautiful, exciting garden, there's nothing for it: you'll have to combine roses with other plants. That's not just for aesthetic reasons, but also because it's good for roses to be in mixed company. Roses that are too close together get fungal diseases more frequently than roses that also have other plants in between.

One thing to keep in mind when combining roses with perennial plants is the location. Roses like sun, water and nutritious soil. So it's pointless combining them with shade plants such as ferns or skimmias. It's also important that the surrounding plants aren't too close to the rose. Make sure to leave 25cm around the plant, so that the soil can be dug over and fertilised.

Perennial plants that go with roses are *Echinacea* varieties, giant hyssops (*Agastache*), foxgloves (*Digitalis*), lady's mantle (*Alchemilla mollis*), *Helenium*, black-eyed Susans (*Rudbeckia*), *Geranium* 'Rozanne', beardtongues (*Penstemon*), goldenrods (*Solidago*), phlox and lamb's ear (*Stachys*). Herbs also make good neighbours. A 'classic' companion for roses is lavender, which is said to keep aphids and ants at bay. If you want plants that look like lavender in terms of colour and growth, you can consider woodland sage (*Salvia nemorosa*), lilac sage (*Salvia verticillata*) or catmint (*Nepeta*). But rosemary, dill, thyme and alliums also go well with roses. As do ornamental grasses, which give a playful touch to the often somewhat austere roses. They are also useful when you have standard roses: if you plant ornamental grasses around the standard rose, you don't have to look at that bare stem anymore.

If roses and perennial plants are in a border together, it's nice if the roses stick out over the other plants. You can do this if you surround the rose with smaller plants such as *Verbena bonariensis* 'Lollipop' or *Geranium macrorrhizum*. A bit smaller and more tolerant of the sun is *Geranium x cantabrigiense*. Another candidate is *Geranium endressii* 'Wargrave Pink', a low cranesbill that dies off in the winter but sprouts again in the spring. Other plants that grow close to the ground are common soapwort (*Saponaria*), Caucasian crosswort (*Phuopsis stylosa*) and carnations.

If you like a wild, natural-looking garden, wild roses are a must. Perennial plants and grasses that have a wild touch fit well in such a garden: for instance, try globe thistles (*Echinops*), larkspur (*Delphinium*), sunflower (*Helianthus*), pink gaura (*Gaura lindheimeri*) and grasses such as blue oat grass (*Helictotrichon sempervirens*), spiky fescue (*Festuca gautieri*) and blue fescue (*Festuca glauca*). And if you love sowing your own seeds, combine the roses with annual plants such as *Cosmos bipinnatus*, snapdragons (*Antirrhinum*), love-in-a-mist (*Nigella*) or common poppies (*Papaver rhoeas*).

Books and magazines will tell you that you have to match the colours and texture of the foliage and flowers. Honestly speaking, I find this quite meaningless. Because why can't one plant be next to another plant, just because their colours don't match? With the result that blue and yellow is OK, but red and yellow is absolutely unacceptable? Who decides that? You yourself, surely? One person might want a garden with soft transitions, while someone else isn't satisfied until the colours burst out of the ground. Whatever makes you happy...

Bee and insect friendly

On the De Bierkreek website, you can use the 'bee and insect friendly' filter to see which roses produce nectar or have recognisable pollen stamens. These are 'clean' roses that are good for wild bees and other insects such as hoverflies, lacewings and parasitic wasps.
Their larvae are the main enemies of aphids.

Pollen

When a honey bee lands on a flower, the pollen spreads all over the hairs on its body. It uses its hairy legs to brush the pollen onto its hind legs, where it ends up in a pollen sac. Then the bee takes the pollen to the bee hive and deposits it in a cell where juvenile bees receive the pollen, which is their food.

BIODIVERSITY

If you plant one or more roses in your garden, you can bet that insects and birds will have found them in no time. If you were to write down what benefits roses have for animals, the list would look like this:

— They give birds, hedgehogs and other small animals a place to shelter all year round.
— From May until autumn, they provide pollen for bees, bumblebees and other insects. The insects are attracted to the scent from a great distance.
— Birds pick caterpillars and aphids off the rose plants.
— The flowers are followed by rose hips. Greenfinches and goldfinches pick out the seeds, while thrushes, blackbirds, fieldfares and redwings swallow the hips whole.

But roses do even more for the animal kingdom around them. If they get attacked by aphids, this attracts ladybirds, lacewings and aphids' other natural enemies. And in turn, the birds feed on those. There are also garden roses that serve as a host plant for some moths, such as the black-spotted chestnut moth (which is actually a butterfly!) and the barred yellow moth.

Bees

Roses have so little nectar that bees and bumblebees don't have much use for it in terms of making honey. Despite that, they flock to roses. That's because what roses *do* have is protein-rich pollen that bees and bumblebees use for feeding their offspring.

Bees mainly visit single and semi-full rose flowers. These blooms have an open structure and the pollen is there for the taking. That doesn't work as well with the full blooms, with the petals all packed close together. These flowers are only also visited by bees when they are faded and have opened up more.

In the twentieth century, very full blooms were in fashion. Whether the flowers were attractive for bees and butterflies was not a consideration back then. This is only changing now as we become more aware of the decline in bee populations—among wild bees in particular—and realise they desperately need protection. For that reason, more people want garden plants that these insects can benefit from. Modern rose breeders are responding to that demand by releasing more single-flower and semi-full roses. Through the 'Nektar Garten' collection, the German rose grower Kordes offers cluster and dwarf roses that they claim wild bees, bumblebees and some butterflies flock to. Fellow rose grower Tantau named their bee-friendly roses 'Bienenweide' (bees' meadow), available in the Netherlands under the name 'Bijenweelde'.

There are also Dutch rose growers who focus on the welfare of bees and other insects. One of the best known is the organic rose nursery De Bierkreek in Biervliet. On their website, they give a cautionary warning: if a rose has a label with a picture of a bee or the words 'Bee Friendly', don't automatically assume that it is actually a rose that attracts bees. You should also check to see if there's a green or black leaf (the European organic quality label). Only then can you be certain that the rose is 'clean' and has not been treated with pesticides.

Wild, native varieties such as the dog rose (*Rosa canina*), burnet rose (*Rosa pimpinellifolia*), wrinkled rose (*Rosa rugosa*) and field rose (*Rosa arvensis*) in particular attract wild bees, hoverflies and other insects. If you're looking for a climbing rose that attracts bees and bumblebees, you could consider the *Rosa* 'Perennial Blue', or the ramblers 'Bobbie James', 'Kiftsgate' and 'Rambling Rector'.

1. HOVERFLY ON *ROSA* 'BRISE PARFUM'
2. BUMBLE BEE ON *ROSA* 'SCHNEEWITTCHEN'
3. HONEY BEES ON *ROSA* 'MIND GAMES'

PUBLIC GREENERY

The term 'public greenery' says what it is: the greenery planted in public spaces. This means parks, public gardens, roundabouts, roadside verges, roofs and walls.

Not all plants are suitable for places that are open to anyone. You shouldn't use fragile plants, of course. People traipse across the plants, children retrieve their footballs and dogs do what dogs do when they're taken out for a walk. What you need are sturdy plants that can cope with rough treatment. In the past, impenetrable shrubs such as barberry were often chosen, but recently more and more perennial plants have been appearing in public green spaces. With their colourful flowers, they brighten up the area and ensure that bees, bumblebees, hoverflies and other insects are also catered for. Which is good for biodiversity. And well... when it comes to colourful flowers and bees, what plant first comes to mind? That's right, the rose!

Now you may be thinking, aren't roses difficult plants that often get sick and need pruning regularly? Sure, that used to be the case, but the newest varieties are strong, healthy shrubs that don't need a lot of care. And if you want to play completely safe, you can opt for wild roses. They are indestructible and also have the single flowers that bees and other insects love.

Roses are also known as lively plants that are easy to combine with other shrubs, ornamental grasses and perennial plants. And what other plant blooms as long as the rose? There are repeat-flowering roses that keep going from May until the first overnight frost. If you let them finish flowering without removing the wilted flowers, the shrubs end up full of rose hips that birds will feed on during the winter.

Roses have so many growth forms that you can choose a suitable variety for every environment. You can have a shrub rose for a park or public garden, a groundcover rose for a roundabout and a climbing rose for a wall. Groundcover roses are low rose shrubs that extend outwards so much that they can cover a large area within a short time. Hardly any

ROSA 'BLANC DOUBLE DE COUBERT'

weeds can get through them. They bloom from May until well into the autumn. As for climbing roses, research has shown that building facades covered with greenery dampen noise, reduce summer heat and improve air quality. When planting greenery in public spaces, the conditions such as the soil type must be taken into account. The only soil type that roses have a hard time with is wet peaty soil. They feel perfectly at home in the other kinds of soil that can be found in the Netherlands. In coastal areas with poor sandy soil, you can consider the burnet rose (*Rosa pimpinellifolia*). Wrinkled roses (*Rosa rugosa*) are roses that need very little extra care and aren't afraid of a bit of wind. Good rugosa roses are 'Alba', 'Blanc Double de Coubert', Fru Dagmar Hastrup', 'Roseraie de l'Hay', 'Rubra', 'Scabrosa' and 'Schneezwerg'.

It should be said, though, that the wrinkled rose has become a problem in the dunes in particular. The shrub spreads both through its root shoots and its seeds. Birds eat the rose hips, and then spread the seeds across large distances. As a result, the variety can quickly start dominating large areas. Finally, there is the issue of pruning, which people always make a thing of in the case of roses. But there's no need for that. If you don't prune roses for a few years, they just keep flowering. Most groundcover roses and hybrid moschatas only need to be pruned back every three to five years. You can do this by cutting them back to 25cm above the ground in March with a flail mower or mowing robot.

Several growers and breeders have developed lines of roses that are exceptionally suitable for public green spaces. For example, Boot & Dart Boomkwekerijen has a selection in their Fleur robust package. They are rose bushes grown on their own roots, which means that they can be pruned mechanically—only necessary once every three years—right back to 20cm above the ground. An additional advantage of these shrubs is that they tolerate salt, so they can also be planted alongside a through road. Two of these roses—'Rote Hannover' and 'Polo'—have received the ADR designation (see page 80). 'Rote Hannover' is a broad, compact shrub with glossy dark green leaves that turn orangey yellow in the autumn. The single flowers are red. 'Polo' is a groundcover rose with single deep red flowers and dark green leaves that remain until well into the autumn, so weeds get little chance to grow.

Other roses that are suitable for city centres, parks and industrial estates are the Pavement roses from the City·flor product range. They were grafted and grow on their own roots, so there are no irregular suckers and they tolerate mechanical pruning, for example with a hedge trimmer. These roses were selected to cope with less favourable circumstances such as poor soil, road salt, exhaust fumes and shady conditions that you mainly find in tree beds, on streets, roundabouts and slopes and in planters.

A relatively new group is the Noack Flower Carpet Roses. They are robust groundcover roses that aren't bothered by fungi such as mildew and black spot. An old favourite is 'Bonica 82' with fine pink, full flowers in clusters. This variety is particularly hardy and resistant to road salt. It's one of the best rose shrubs for roadsides, on the street side of a garden, in the central reservations of big roads and even in coastal areas.

PAVEMENT-ROSE *ROSA* 'STRANDPAREL
AMRUM' FROM THE CITY-FLOR RANGE

THE JOY OF
roses

CARING
FOR ROSES

ANTOINE VESTIER
PORTRAIT OF A LADY PICKING A ROSE (1791)

BALTHASAR VAN DER AST
STILL LIFE WITH ROSE AND IRIS
(CA. 1625)

Caring for roses

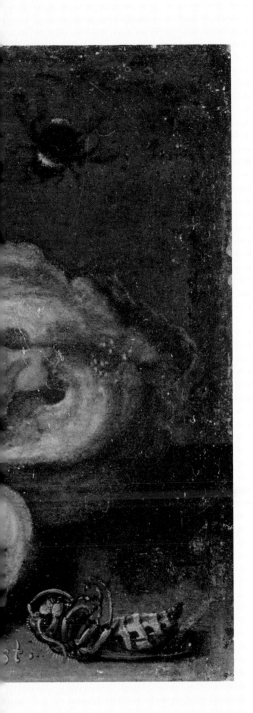

Roses are—honestly—no more difficult than other plants

Most people love plants, especially when they have flowers. Those are the kinds of plants they want in their gardens. Geraniums, hydrangeas, lavender... it doesn't matter what. But no roses, please! I've met dedicated rose lovers who told me that they only started growing roses later in life. They were too afraid before, because they thought they wouldn't be able to keep those difficult roses alive.

Of course, it's useful to know what you need to do to keep a plant healthy and looking good, but that applies to all plants. And roses are—honestly—no more difficult than other plants. The idea that they are tricky miracles comes from the time when they were indeed like that. A rose grower once told me the story. "In the past," he said, "we only had wild roses. They had single flowers and had finished blooming after about four weeks. Until the eighteenth century everyone was perfectly happy with these short-flowering roses. But then they found a rose in China that flowered all summer. That rose was brought to Europe by ship and it brought us nothing by trouble. If I'd been on that ship, I'd have thrown it overboard. Everyone wanted that repeat-flowering Chinese miracle rose, so it was crossed so often that it became exhausted. But not to worry: the rose was grafted onto a strong root system, and then the crossing and selecting carried on as before. But the Chinese rose turned out to be extremely susceptible to problems such as black spot, mildew and rust. And that property was passed on to all the succeeding generations. That's how the Chinese rose, which all of our repeat-flowering roses are descended from, gave the rose a bad name."

It's unfortunate that this history continues to haunt the rose. There are undoubtedly still roses that are susceptible to diseases, but breeders have been working on selecting resilient roses for so long that there is plenty of choice in robust roses that no more care than geraniums and lavender.

NUTRITION

Roses grow fast and flower abundantly, so they need nutrients. This also gives them more resistance against diseases. Very robust varieties such as wild roses can go a long time without extra nutrients, but all other roses need to be fed.

When

Most roses only need fertiliser twice a year: in March and in June. Repeat-flowering roses in particular need these two doses. Single-flowering bush roses appreciate an extra treatment in August/September. Potted roses need fertiliser three or four times per year. In the winter you can give your garden roses a layer of compost, which can be dug in in the spring.

With what

The best fertiliser for roses is old farmyard manure or organic manure pellets, but a special fertiliser for roses works just as well. It remains active for about three months. Sprinkle the fertiliser at the foot of the rose, preferably before a rainy period, and rake it in lightly. The easiest way to feed roses is the 'Healthy Start' fertiliser, which remains active all year. It comes in the form of tablets that you press into the soil around the plants. This gives them organic fertiliser, humic acids and beneficial soil bacteria.

WATERING ROSES DURING PROLONGED DROUGHT

Heat and drought have little effect on well-rooted roses. Young and newly planted roses do need a lot of water, though, to become properly established. During prolonged drought, you can give additional water. Giving the rose a lot of water in one go is better than a little bit every day. Pour the water over the soil, not the plant.

DEAD-HEADING

In repeat-flowering roses, dead-head all the faded flowers regularly through to mid-September. If you don't, the plant will put all its energy into creating hips, which contain the seeds that are necessary for the most important task a plant has, namely reproduction. As long as you keep dead-heading the flowers, the plant keeps producing new flowers to attract insects.

SUCKERS

Most roses have been T-budded (= grafted) onto the rootstock of a wild rose. Breeders do this to give the grafted rose a strong base. But one drawback of this approach is that the wild rootstock will keep producing shoots itself that grow into branches with leaves. These branches can be recognised because they come out of the ground. They also have more thorns and leaves. The leaves are usually light green and finer than those of the T-budded rose. You don't want suckers like that, because they divert nutrients away from the grafted rose. Dig away the soil and check that this branch is indeed a sucker from below the thick bud union. If it is, tear the sucker off the stem by pulling it downwards. Don't prune it and don't cut it away with a knife, as it will just sprout again.

1.   2.   3.

1.   ORGANIC ROSE FERTILISER   4.   DEAD-HEADING ROSES WITH SECATEURS
2.   WELL-ROTTED STABLE MANURE   5.   SUCKER
3.   'HEALTHY START' FERTILISER   6.   BUCKET OF DEAD-HEADED ROSES
     TABLET

1. *ROSA* 'SALLY HOLMES' WITH
    EUPHORBIA (*EUPHORBIA*
    CHARACIAS) AND ERIGERON
    (*ERIGERON KARVINSKIANUS*)
2. CLIMBING ROSE TRAINED
    HORIZONTALLY ALONG A WALL
3. *ROSA* 'CONSTANCE SPRY'
4. *ROSA* 'NEW DAWN'
5. *ROSA* 'GERTRUDE JEKYLL'

SUPPORTING AND GUIDING CLIMBING AND RAMBLING ROSES

Climbing roses take up little space and are ideal for covering something ugly—a wall, fence or an old bare tree. They are subdivided into climbing roses and ramblers. Climbing roses get 3-4m tall at most, whereas the long, flexible branches of ramblers can easily reach 15m. Most climbing roses flower all summer, while rambling roses—with a few exceptions— only flower for about four weeks. But when they do, they do it exuberantly, with clusters full of flowers smaller than those of climbing roses. Examples of repeat-flowering rambling roses are 'Mme Isaac Pereire' and 'New Dawn'.

Climbing roses aren't genuine climbing plants: they grow upwards but they have no clinging roots, so they need support from a trellis against a wall, a rose arch, an arbour or pergola, an obelisk or pyramid, a fence or a tree.

Wall

The best wall for climbing roses is one facing the southwest, where the plant gets a lot of sun and rainwater. A climbing rose climbing up a wall needs to be tied to a grid of strong (plasticised) steel wire or steel cables, or to a wooden slatted trellis. The height and width of the trellis depend on how vigorous the growth of the climbing plant is, but it must be at least 2m tall and just as wide.

The roses need a plant hole of at least 40 x 40cm. Make sure there is at least 15cm space between the wall and the slatted trellis, to allow wind to pass and the leaves to dry more easily. Take down the young shoots that try to grow upwards and tie them horizontally to a support. This way, the buds will sprout along the whole length of the branch. It's better not to put the rose against a southern wall, because it can get too hot there.

Roses need at least four hours of sun every day to grow and bloom well. Despite that, there are a few climbing roses that also do well against a northern wall, as long as the spot gets enough light. Examples are 'Albéric Barbier', 'Albertine', 'Climbing Iceberg', 'Félicité et Perpétué', 'Guirlande d'Amour', 'Mermaid', 'New Dawn', 'Parkdirektor Riggers', 'The Pilgrim' and 'Veilchenblau'.

Suitable roses for a small wall: 'Cascade' (syn. 'Nordina'), 'Laguna', 'Lichtkönigin Lucia', 'Little Rambler', 'Open Arms', 'Porcelaine de Chine' and 'Westerland'.

Rose arch

Rose arches can be found in all shapes and sizes, from very large to something suitable for a small garden. Use one made from sustainable material. If you choose iron, make sure it has received an anti-rust treatment. If you prefer wood, go for ecological hardwood or wood that has been thermally modified for durability, or treat it beforehand with an ecological varnish. If you buy tropical hardwood, make sure it's certified, for example with an FSC or PEFC label, which indicates sustainable forest management.

To cover a rose arch, you can plant climbers that don't grow very fast. To prevent a situation where all the flowers end up at the top after a while, bend the main branches halfway and tie them to the arch horizontally using binding tube. They then form new side branches with many flowers.

Nice roses for a rose arch are 'Blaze Superior' and 'Kiss me Kate'.

Arbour or pergola

Arbours or pergolas are very suitable for roses because they get plenty of air. For this you need roses with flexible branches that grow fast, get at least 4m tall and preferably flower from June to September.

Suitable roses are 'Albertine', 'New Dawn', 'Pippin' and 'Swan Lake'.

Obelisk or pyramid

A rambler or climbing rose with slightly stiffer branches, can be guided against a round, straight or pyramidal obelisk. Take a sturdy climbing support made from sustainable material such as wrought iron or ecological hardwood. There are also ready-made plastic ones for sale. The pyramids should preferably be about 3m tall and 1.0-1.5m wide at ground level. Make sure the supports are inserted at least 40cm into the ground. In a windy location, you can additionally anchor the bottom 20cm in stabilised sand. This material consists of concrete sand with 10 per cent concrete, giving the soil stability, providing a firmer substrate. The pyramids should have enough cross-connections for you to tie the rose's branches to.

Good options are 'Felicia', 'Florentina', 'John Davis' and 'Paul Transon'.

Against fencing

Roses that don't get taller than 2m can also climb up fencing, for example made of a wire mesh. Have a look at 'Pink Magic' and 'White Magic', 'Robusta', 'Souvenir de Louis Lens' or 'Veilchenblau'.

In trees

Roses can grow in any deciduous tree, but preferably not in evergreens such as pines and fir trees, because the rose will suffer from the lack of light. If you want to combine roses with fruit trees that grow relatively slowly, such as peach, apricot or plum trees, choose roses that also don't grow that fast. Those trees need a lot of light to produce fruits. Keep an eye out for possible overgrowth and take pruning shears to your roses every year.

The rambler 'Adélaïde d'Orléans' doesn't grow fast, which makes it easy to guide. They get about 6m tall, making them suitable for small trees. 'Albéric Barbier' tolerates semi-shade and easily reaches 6m or more. 'Louis' Rambler' gets 7-8m tall and flowers in June and July with buds that open as light yellow and finish flowering as white. 'Wedding Day' tolerates poor soil and shade.

Combinations with other climbing plants

You can combine climbing roses with other climbers, on the condition that they don't take away light and don't suffocate or smother the roses. Climbing plants that roses get along well with are jasmine (*Jasminum officinale*) and clematis (except for a strong grower like *Clematis montana*). Climbing plants that don't go well with roses are honeysuckles (*Lonicera*), Wisteria, silver lace vine (*Fallopia aubertii*), Virginia creeper (*Parthenocissus*) and chocolate vine (*Akebia quinata*).

Tips for roses in trees

— Always plant the rose on the sunny side, never on the shadow side of a tree. They don't get enough light there. The south-west side is the best: roses get the most water and sunlight there.

— For large trees, choose a rose that also does well in semi-shade.

— Don't plant roses and young trees at the same time. Give the trees a head start of at least five years, especially in the case of a standard fruit tree. Some roses grow so fast and get so voluminous that they can smother a young tree.

— Plant the rose 1m away from the trunk and guide it towards the tree diagonally.

— Tie the rose to the trunk with a flexible binding tube. Keep doing that until the rose reaches the canopy. Then it will find enough support itself.

— Give climbing roses in trees organic (rose) fertiliser at least twice a year, in March and in June. Roses need extra energy to compete with the trees.

— Prune roses in young or small fruit trees every year in March. This way the tree and its fruits get enough light and sun.

BIRCH WITH A CLIMBING ROSE

Tying with binding tube

Tie the climbing rose to a support. Keep doing this, otherwise the branches that have continued growing will droop. Use binding tube, an elastic plastic wire that's hollow on the inside. It can be used to tie the branches without damaging them. Binding tube is easy to tie, expands as the branches get thicker, and lasts for years.

Don't tie roses with regular cord, raffia or plasticised iron wire. Regular cord cuts them, raffia decays quickly and plasticised iron wire cuts off the sap flow, depriving the roses of nutrition. Tie the branches loosely, in a figure of eight. Keep in mind that the branches get thicker each year, so make sure to leave some slack. Guide the branches horizontally as much as possible: this slows down the growth and promotes flowering. Horizontal branches get a lot more side shoots (and therefore more flowers) than vertical branches. If you let the rose do its thing, you get loads of flowers at the top while the bottom remains bare.

Apple trees

Roses that are susceptible to mildew can transmit it to equally susceptible apple varieties. That's why you should only plant strong and healthy roses to climb up apple trees.

PRUNING

Throughout the Netherlands, courses on pruning roses are given each spring. These courses are always packed. Pruning roses is apparently so complicated that we don't dare to do it until we have taken a course.

But why is it so difficult? Because most garden books need thirty pages to explain how to do it—and in particular how not to do it? Or because there are so many rose varieties, and we think each variety needs a different treatment? But how come a pruning course never takes more than an hour? And after that hour, you grab your pruning shears in relief and clip all the roses in your garden as if you've been doing it your whole life?

If you choose the path of least resistance, you simply do nothing. But that's not recommended, because most roses appreciate pruning. A pruning session for a rose is like a Botox treatment for us: a rejuvenating treatment. Removing old branches gives new shoots a chance and the rose is encouraged to bloom. Thinned shrubs have the added benefit of wind blowing through the plant, drying wet leaves out more quickly and reducing the chances of fungal diseases.

The most important rule when pruning roses is that whatever you do, you can't go wrong. No matter how much you cut away, they'll always recover. After these reassuring words, let's have a look at which roses like being pruned and which don't.

Single-flowering roses

We start with the roses that flower for about four weeks because they are the easiest. These include wild roses, old garden roses, many ramblers and most moss roses—and they don't actually need to be pruned. If you want to make space or if the tangle of branches annoys you, you can remove old or weak branches immediately after flowering—in July or August.

Repeat-flowering roses

Most roses are repeat-flowering roses. These are roses that start flowering in June and—with or without a short break—keep going until the first overnight frost. These roses are pruned in March, when the sap flow has started and the buds begin to swell.

— **Grandiflora roses (hybrid tea) and cluster roses**

Leave three or four strong branches and cut all other branches down to the ground. Then prune the three or four remaining branches back to 10-15cm from the ground, or right above the third bud from the ground. Clipping a rose almost down to the ground sounds scary, but there's a logic to it. The shorter the branches are, the less energy the rose needs to devote to the buds. If you leave those branches long, only the top two buds will sprout. The rest will remain 'dormant' with the result that you get a long, bare branch with flowers only at the top.

— **Shrub roses**

Prune all branches back to 5-10cm above the ground. Each branch will have two or three buds remaining.

— **Standard roses**

These are shrub roses grafted onto a stem. They are pruned the same way as shrub roses.

— **Miniature roses**

These are tiny shrub roses that you only need to shorten a little bit.

— **Bush roses**

Bush roses get a bit larger and more tangled than shrub roses. You only have to prune them every three to four years, between December and March. First, remove the dead, infected and damaged branches. Then cut most of the oldest branches (those with a brownish colour) down to the ground. Also remove a few branches from the centre for that essential air circulation.

— **English (Austin) roses**

If you prune the branches of an English rose to half their length, the plant will get more leaves and fewer (but larger) flowers. If you prune them less severely and only cut off a third of the branches, the shrub will get more (but smaller) flowers.

— **Groundcover roses**

These grow slowly and therefore only need to be clipped once every three to five years, until a stump of 10-15cm remains. You can do this with a hedge trimmer.

— **Climbing roses**

You don't start pruning a climbing rose until it is two or three years old. You can do this between December and March. Pruning in the winter encourages the climbing rose to create new branches with strong shoots from buds at the bottom of the plant.

1. PRUNING SHRUB ROSES
2. PRUNING STANDARD ROSES
3. CUTTING DEAD WOOD FROM
   A ROSE BUSH

First, remove all dead branches and thin shoots. In climbing roses, the flowers grow on side shoots off the main branches. Leave those main branches alone and focus on the side branches. Prune them down to a few centimetres, so that two or three healthy buds remain on each branch.

Remove one of the main branches every few years. If the climbing rose is attached to a trellis along the wall, make sure there are five main branches. Bend those branches down so that they become somewhat horizontal and tie them to the trellis with binding tube. Cut away everything that sticks outwards from the wall, ignoring outer eyes. The flowers will grow towards the light, as the shrub only has one route because of the wall. If any side branches are sticking out from the horizontal branches, cut them back so far that they become like pegs. These will grow young shoots again.

A rambler can be allowed to do its thing, because it flowers even if you don't prune it. If you like a neat look, you can remove dead branches and parts that have finished flowering every now and then. If the rambler gets a bit too wild, prune a few of the oldest branches that have flowered down to the ground immediately after the rose has finished flowering—from the end of July to early August. Don't be afraid: they'll grow back again spontaneously.

— **Weeping roses**

These are climbing roses on a stem. You don't need to do much, except remove old and dead wood. If you feel an irresistible urge to get clipping, prune it like it's a climbing rose.

1. PRUNING A CLIMBING ROSE
2. PRUNING ABOVE THE EYE

1. EYE PRUNED TOO SHORT
2. CORRECTLY PRUNED EYE
3. PRUNED TOO FAR FROM
   THE EYE

1.   2.   3.

Before you start pruning

Before you start actually pruning, first remove all old, dead and damaged branches. Always cut the stem diagonally, so that the rainwater can flow off the wound. And give the roses a handful of organic fertiliser after pruning them.

What is an eye?

An eye is a bud that a new shoot grows from. An 'outer eye' is a bud that points outwards. According to the rules, you should always prune above the outer eye, because the new rose branches then grow outwards, towards the light. But if you prune haphazardly, without paying attention to the outer eyes, the branch will follow its instinct, which is to grow in the direction of the sun.

Stem holders and telescopes

There are rose shears with a stem holder that holds onto the stem that has just been cut so that it doesn't fall to the ground. You can use these secateurs to prune without having to grab the thorny branch. There are also rose shears with a telescopic arm, letting you keep a safe distance from the thorns.

Keep your secateurs sharp and clean

If you use blunt secateurs (pruning shears), they can tear the stem, making the pruning wound larger than it needs to be. So you should always work with sharp pruning shears. Clean them afterwards with fine sandpaper and some oil. And make sure the secateurs are regularly disinfected with methylated spirits or alcohol. Especially if you cut branches that look diseased, it's best not to move on to the next rose immediately. Get a bottle of 70 per cent alcohol from the chemist, put some on a cloth and rub it over the blades of the pruning shears.

"I PRUNE ALMOST EVERY DAY, BECAUSE JUST LIKE IN A JUNGLE I NEED TO KEEP THE PATH CLEAR"

Roger Willeghems

ROSE LOVER

Roger Willeghems admits he has had a love-hate relationship with roses for half his life. "As a child, we had a small garden. I did love flowers and plants, but I hated roses. I was a real socialist, and to me roses were a symbol of the bourgeoisie. I also associated roses with the rich nobility because in the nineteenth century, only the aristocracy and the bourgeoisie were able to buy roses for their parks and gardens. Roses were usually too expensive for ordinary people."

"In the 1990s I used to cycle a lot; I was a tour cyclist. Whenever my cycling friends saw my front garden, they'd say, 'Look, a serious cyclist lives here.' Because that front garden of mine looked terrible! All the cycling meant I had no time for it. It wasn't until the mid-1990s when I gave up cycling that I took up gardening seriously. I visited a garden centre to buy plants and smelled an amazing fragrance. It came from *Rosa* 'William Shakespeare', an English rose. I was sold immediately and came home with three roses: 'Mary Rose', 'William Shakespeare' and 'Winchester Cathedral'. And my principles, yeah, I had to abandon them. Didn't the French and Belgian socialists have the rose as their symbol? And the Dutch socialists too? Nice. And nowadays roses are sold for a democratic price; anyone can buy a rose. So they're no longer elitist. And that's how I turned from a rose hater into a rose lover.

I wanted fragrant, healthy, repeat-flowering roses and at the time this meant David Austin's English roses. I bought a few of them. In addition to 'William Shakespeare' and 'Winchester Cathedral', I also had 'Fisherman's Friend', 'Golden Celebration', 'Graham Thomas' and others. And 'Gertrude Jekyll', a skimpy plant, but the flowers and the scent are amazing.

In the end it didn't work out with those roses; my soil wasn't good enough. I lived in Tervuren, in a recently built house. It had a basement, and the dead, heavy clay soil that was excavated to construct that basement had just been dumped in the garden. I planted my roses in that soil, and they soon died due to my incompetence. The rose literature taught me that the ideal rose soil is one third of the existing soil, supplemented with one third river sand and one third compost.

After my infatuation for English roses my passion expanded to include botanic and Old roses and hybrid moschatas. Before I became passionate about roses, I kept bees. To help the bees get plenty of nectar and pollen I planted fruit trees in my garden. When I then started with roses, I thought, 'I can't possibly cut down all these trees?' Which is how I came up with the idea of letting climbing roses grow into those

trees. I got ramblers. I still think the best one is 'Madame Alfred Carrière'.

My garden of 1,500m2 is full of climbers and ramblers. It's a real jungle, with narrow paths. I can almost walk through it with my eyes closed, but anyone else would get hopelessly entangled in the prickly branches and need a machete to

ROSA 'MADAME ALFRED CARRIÈRE'

make progress and get out. I don't prune. No, that's a joke! What I mean is that I don't prune in the regular period, in March. I prune a bit almost every day, because just like in a jungle I need to keep the paths clear. I can't stand the sight of a dead branch—it has to go. And when the roses start growing and blooming, the added weight makes them droop and I have to keep clearing the path. In the autumn, storm winds can harm the roses. Throughout the winter, I take the time to remove dead branches. I need that time, because I don't want to become a slave to my own garden."

On his patio he cherishes Chinese roses. "These are my darlings. Roses like *Rosa* 'Comtesse du Cayla', *Rosa* 'Sophie's Perpetual', 'Perle d'Or' and 'Old Blush China' for example, are the first Chinese roses that were crossed with European roses. They're sensitive to frost, so you need to cover them when it's freezing. But they have something special, they're unique. Delicate red branches, that little flower..." He shows a photo on his phone. "Look, that's a real Picasso, very irregular and very artistic, in my opinion." Sometimes, says Roger, a spontaneous mutation occurs. "We call this a sport. It happened to me once with *Rosa* 'Thalia', a rambler. It normally has white flowers, but pink flowers suddenly appeared on one branch. I cut the branch off and had it T-budded by the breeder Lens Roses. And now I have *Rosa* 'Rogers Thalia' with pink flowers. It isn't available for sale because rambling roses are hardly sold anymore."

He mainly has wild and Old roses, he says. "I love the natural look. With the continuous breeding, roses have declined in quality. Small roses are popular now, because our gardens keep getting smaller. Nobody can now say they don't have room for roses because there's always room for something like 'Cutie Pie'. That's a mini rose, yes, even a micro rose that you can put on the table. It doesn't get taller than 15cm, doesn't have thorns and doesn't have to be pruned."

I ask Roger if there are roses that are resistant to diseases. "Do you never get a cold?" he retorts. "People always make such a fuss about it. They often tell me that they don't want roses in their garden because roses always get diseases. If they see one black spot on a single leaf, they immediately panic. But should roses be banished from the garden because of this? No! The only rose that never gets sick is a plastic one."

ROGER WILLEGHEMS
Oudergemseweg 92, B-3080 Tervuren, Belgium.
E-mail: roger@willeghems.be

1. *ROSA* 'FRANCIS E. LESTER'
2. *ROSA* 'WILDERODE'

PROTECTION AGAINST FROST

Adding soil

The bud union is the most fragile part of a rose. It's normally about 5cm underground, but after a few years the bud union moves up and is exposed again. That's why you should protect the roses against frost by piling up soil. You do this by placing a pile of garden soil or compost around the foot of the rose in the autumn. You can remove that pile in March.

Standard rose

In standard roses, the fragile bud union is located at the end of the stem. It's the thickened part where the branches come out of the stem and in this case, that point is high above the ground, so of course it can't be covered by piling up soil. You can protect a standard rose against frost by binding something around the bud union. If you are advised to pull a plastic bag around the branches and tie it closed around the stem, let that advice go in one ear and out the other. This bag can make the rose so warm that shoots start sprouting. Those shoots then dry out as soon as you remove the bag. There's a better way of protecting the standard rose against frost: pack the bud union by tying bundles of straw or pine branches around it.

Pot

You can put roses in pots and planters that are sensitive to frost in the garage, shed, utility room or the attic. If you don't have such spaces, put the pots in a place where they are sheltered from cold wind. Wrap jute or protective mats of sheep's wool around the pot and tie another jute cloth or felt cloth around it. Don't let the root clump dry out. Remove the protection in mid-March, and give the rose a pruning session and a lot of organic fertiliser or rose fertiliser.

1. ROSE SHRUB WITH HILLOCK OF GARDEN SOIL
2. GRAFTING LOCATION OF STANDARD ROSE PACKED IN STRAW
3. POT WRAPPED IN WOOL
4. POT WRAPPED IN JUTE

2.

THE JOY OF
roses

PROPAGATING
ROSES

Propagating roses

*It's simple to make more roses
from one you already have*

For flexible, herbaceous rose cuttings, late spring or early summer is
a good moment for taking cuttings. Woody cuttings can best be taken
between mid-October and mid-November. They take root more slowly.

LAYERING

The easiest way of 'creating' a new rose bush is by layering it. You can layer the plant by bending a flexible branch towards the ground. You'll have the most success with climbing roses and cluster roses with strong and flexible one-year-old wood, and with wild roses grown on their own roots, i.e. that aren't T-budded onto rootstock.

Choose a one-year-old branch—preferably in September. Wound the branch by making a few long incisions in the bark in the place where it goes into the ground. It will form roots at that point. Make a 5cm-deep groove, put the branch in it and hold the branch in place with a clamp or a piece of iron wire. Cover the groove with potting compost and attach the end of the branch to a bamboo stick. One year later, you'll have a well-rooted plant that you can cut off the mother bush and plant the new one somewhere else. Your new rose bush has the same genetic properties as the mother plant.

CUTTINGS

Growers are increasingly taking cuttings of roses instead of T-budding them. A benefit of cuttings is that you don't need experienced T-budders. The roses also have a shorter growth period and are available all year round, in different sizes. The only downside is that roses cultivated from cuttings are a bit more vulnerable in harsh winters.

Taking cuttings is almost as easy as layering. Basically, you cut off branches from a rose bush and stick them into the ground. It doesn't always work because not all rose varieties are suitable for taking cuttings. As with layering, climbing roses and cluster roses (*polyantha*) have the best chance of success. A rose cultivated from a cutting is genetically identical to the mother plant, so it will have the same properties. That means you'll know in advance what the new rose will look like.

Taking herbaceous cuttings

Select the rose you want to take cuttings from. Choose long, sturdy shoots that were formed this year. Because they need to go into the ground as quickly as possible after being cut off, it's useful to prepare pots beforehand with four fifths potting compost and one fifth sharp sand or vermiculite. Use sharp pruning shears to cut off a long branch and divide it into 20-25cm lengths. These are the cuttings. Cut the bottom of the cutting horizontally, just below a leaf bud: this will be the bottom. Cut the top of the cutting diagonally,

right above a leaf: this is the top. You now have a cutting that's straight at the bottom and diagonal at the top. This is useful, because now you know which end goes into the soil. Leave the upper leaves, but remove the rest. You can dip the bottom of the cutting in rooting powder to encourage root growth, but it's not really necessary. Stick the cuttings halfway into pots containing potting compost, press the soil down and water the pots. Next, put them in a greenhouse or cover each pot with a plastic bag. Remove that bag every now and then to let air in. Keep the cuttings during the winter in a light, frost-free place and make sure they don't dry out. If leaves grow from the top eyes in the spring, you know they've put down roots.

Taking woody cuttings

Use sharp secateurs to cut off a strong, one-year-old branch. Cut away the upper and lower ends (these have the least developed buds), leaving a 25-30cm cutting with four to five well-developed buds. Cut off the bottom of the cutting horizontally, right under a bud. And cut the top off diagonally, right above a bud. Leave some leaves on the top two buds and remove the rest. Using a sharp knife, make a few incisions in the bark 1-2cm from the bottom where the bottom leaf bud is. This encourages the bark cambium or bark tissue to form roots.

In a sunny spot in the garden, dig a 15cm deep, narrow groove. Fill it with seed and cutting compost and put the cuttings halfway into the soil, so that they're firmly anchored in the ground. Make sure at least two buds are above the ground. Press the soil around the cuttings down firmly and give plenty of water.

They will sprout in the spring. Most cuttings can be dug up after a year and planted in their final spot. If that isn't possible, leave them for another year.

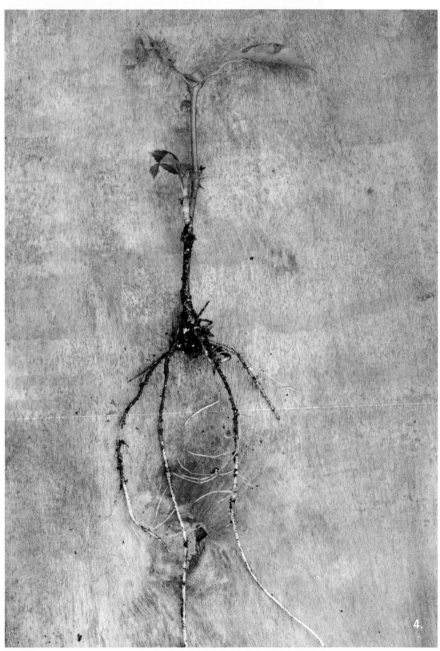

1. LONG STURDY SHOOT
2. DIVIDED INTO PARTS
3. CUTTINGS IN POT
4. SPROUTED CUTTING

1. HIP OF A DOG ROSE
   (*ROSA CANINA*)
2. HIP OF A CHESTNUT ROSE
   (*ROSA ROXBURGHII*)

SOWING

To be able to sow roses, you need rose hips. They contain the seeds, from which roses grow that are usually not true to the variety. This means they can look completely different from their parents. Exceptions to this rule are the wild or botanical roses such as *Rosa canina*, *Rosa rubiginosa*, *Rosa chinensis* and *Rosa rugosa*. Their seedlings usually have the same properties, although the flowers can sometimes have a different colour.

Pluck the hips when they are ripe and leave them to dry indoors for a week. Then cut them open and remove the seeds. To be able to germinate, seeds need a period of frost. You can choose whether that 'frost' happens indoors or outdoors. If you want to put the seeds indoors, put them in the vegetable drawer of the fridge for at least a month at about 4°C. In gardening jargon, this is called stratification. Basically, you mimic the winter conditions that the seeds need to germinate. Afterwards, store the seeds in a cool, frost-free place, in a container with dry white sand to protect them from drying out.

Wait until March and then fill pots or a sowing tray with seed or potting compost. Prick one or two 1cm-deep holes

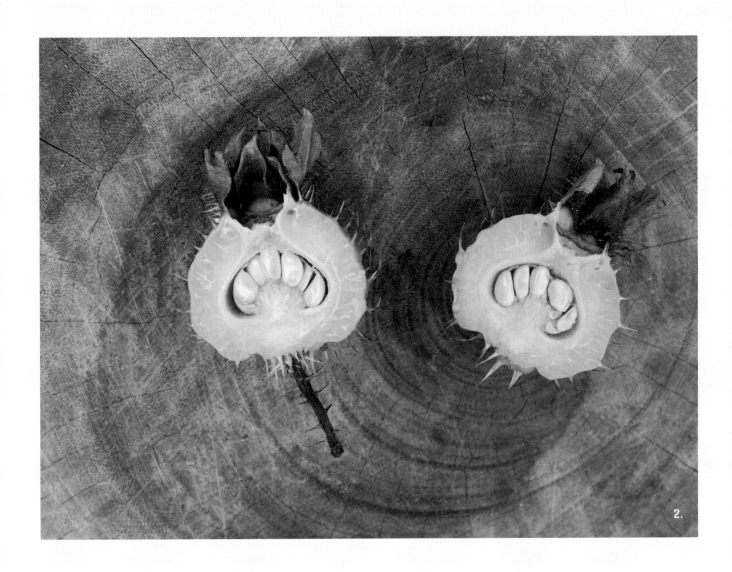

2.

in each section using a pencil, and put a seed in each hole. Cover the hole with soil and press it down again. Give the seeds a little bit of water using a plant spray and put the pots or sowing tray in a light place, at about 15°C. A month later the seeds will germinate and the plants appear. In September you can plant them in the garden. If there are plants that look diseased or mouldy, discard them.

If you want to the seeds to germinate outside, sow them in pots or trays with seed or potting compost and cover them with netting to keep out mice. Leave them outside for the entire winter. When the first seedlings start to germinate,

put them in an unheated room. When the first leaves appear in the spring, give each seedling its own little pot.

If you don't feel like going through the hassle with pots and trays, you can also sow the seeds directly in the garden. In that case you draw 1cm deep rows using the tip of a hoe or rake. Sprinkle a layer of seed or potting compost into each row and put the seeds on top of that, with 5cm in between them. Cover everything with potting compost, press the soil down firmly and moisten it. After four to six weeks the roses will start to germinate. One or two years later, they can be moved to where you want them to end up.

09

DISEASES
AND PESTS

1. POWDERY MILDEW
2. RUST
3. DOWNY MILDEW

Diseases and pests

Diseases often sound worse than they are

Many rose books give a lot of attention to the countless scary diseases and pests roses can get. If you ever wanted to plant a rose in your garden, you'll have second thoughts after reading such a book. That's why a word of comfort is in order: those diseases sound worse than they are. It's true that roses were known—and rightly so—as weaklings that you needed to keep alive using every trick at your disposal. This was the case in the days when breeders were so focused on the appearance of the flower that they forgot the rest of the shrub, which meant they paid no attention to resistance against diseases. In that regard, a lot has changed—for the better—in recent years. Although, with the exception of a few wild roses, there are no roses that never get sick. As a rose lover once remarked, "The only rose that never gets sick is a plastic one." And no, you don't want those in your garden.

In wet summers in particular, any roses are susceptible to fungi such as black spot and mildew. Robust roses get just a mild infection that doesn't impede the vigour of their growth and blooming. But if the rose is a bit weaker and if it's also in the wrong place in the wrong soil, then it's likely to suffer. Choosing a rose that is not susceptible to fungi and other problems, or at any rate less susceptible, lets you avoid a lot of trouble. Plant your rose in good soil and make sure it gets enough nutrients. And perhaps the most important tip of all: ask the grower which roses are least susceptible to diseases.

APHIDS

Aphids prefer young leaves. They are often found on the underside of the leaf, where they feed by sucking sap from the plant. The rose doesn't die, but the leaves and buds become deformed. On top of that, the aphids also secrete honeydew, which attracts sooty mould.

Features: A lot of green or pink crawling insects on the buds and the ends of young shoots of your roses.

Control: You can brush the aphids off with your hand or spray them off with a strong jet from a garden hose or plant sprayer. But before you do, remember that aphids have a lot of natural enemies. They feed on aphids or lay an egg inside the insect, which then develops into a larva and then a mature insect, which in turn lays more eggs in aphids. If you remove aphids, you'll disrupt that cycle and you'll get fewer natural enemies in your garden.

Precautions: To attract the natural enemies such as parasitic wasps, lacewings, hoverflies and ladybirds, you can make sure they can find plenty of pollen and honey in your garden. Plant lavender, sage or thyme between the roses. Attract tits, sparrows, robins and blackbirds to your garden by installing nesting boxes.

1. APHIDS
2. POWDERY MILDEW
3. DOWNY MILDEW

1.

MILDEW (POWDERY)

Powdery mildew is caused by the fungus *Sphaerotheca pannosa*. Mildew occurs most commonly during prolonged periods of drought, especially in periods with a lot of morning dew. Climbers that climb against a wall are especially susceptible to it. The disease spreads fast, but is rarely fatal.

Features: The tops of the leaves, the young shoots and the flower buds are covered with a white fungal growth. They become deformed and shrivel away.

Treatment: Cut off the infected plant parts and throw them into the organic waste container. From May to mid-July, you can spray an environmentally friendly agent based on organic fatty acids once every two weeks. If the rose is severely infected, prune it until there are three or four branches left that still have three or four buds. Give the rose 40-50 grams of organic rose fertiliser. It'll sprout again and bloom in a month or two. Cut the infected shrub down to within 30cm of the ground after the last flowers have faded (in October or November).

Precautions: Plant susceptible roses in a sunny and airy spot, where the leaves dry quickly after a rainstorm or morning dew.

MILDEW (DOWNY)

Downy mildew is caused by the fungus *Pseudoperonospora sparsa*. The fungus forms under hot, moist conditions. Young plants in particular get infected.

Features: Downy mildew can be recognised by dirty white or reddish spots on the underside of the rose leaves, which can make them die. The difference between downy and powdery mildew is that in downy mildew the spotting is on the underside of the leaves, and in powdery mildew on the upper side of the leaves.

Treatment: Remove infected leaves and throw them into the organic waste container.

Precautions: Make sure the leaves stay dry when watering.

2.

3.

1. RUST
2. *DIPLOCARPON ROSAE*
3. LADYBIRD LARVA

RUST

Rust is caused by the fungus *Phragmidium mucronatum*. Rust mainly develops in hot and persistently humid weather.
Features: Small orange dots (sporangia) on both sides of the leaves. The leaf turns yellow and falls off. An infection with rust impedes growth and the shrubs will hardly bloom at all.
Treatment: The treatment is the same as for black spot.
Precautions: Only water the soil, and avoid the plant. Make sure you prune the roses regularly, keeping the shrubs airy so that fungi cannot get established as easily.

ROSEBUD ROT

Bud rot affects the flowers, but fortunately it is rare. It can develop in cold, damp weather.
Features: The petals stick together due to a layer of fungus. The bud doesn't open, rots away and falls off.
Precautions: Bud rot affects roses that have many thin petals. Fortunately, most modern roses aren't affected due to their thick petals.

SPIDER MITES

Features: Spider mites are such small, sap-suckling spidery creatures that you can barely see them with the naked eye. They can usually be found on the undersides of leaves, where they suck plant sap. This creates yellow dots that later turn into a yellowish-brown discolouration of the leaf. If the pest spreads, cobwebs appear in the axils of the plants.
Treatment: Spider mites have become resistant to many chemical products, so it's best to treat them organically. Spider mites on roses can be combated using Forni-mite, which contains predatory mites that eat adult spider mites, eggs and nymphs.
Precautions: Choose roses that are less susceptible to spider mites.

2.

COMBAT APHIDS
Use the larvae of lacewings and ladybirds.
www.biogroei.nl
www.greengardener.co.uk/shop/ladybirds-and-lacewings/
https://ladybirdplantcare.co.uk/

3.

BLACK SPOT

Black spot or leaf blotch disease is caused by the fungus *Diplocarpon rosae*. It's mainly active in hot, humid weather. Fortunately, there are roses that are resistant to it. If they are in a windy spot and get enough fertiliser, they will be even more resistant.

Features: The leaves get purple spots that later turn black and then yellow. Severely affected leaves fall off the plant. Blooming stops and the flowers become deformed. If the rose is severely infected, it'll be rather bare by mid-summer and stop blooming. But it won't die.

Treatment: Clean all affected and fallen leaves and throw them into the organic waste container. The spores of the fungi spend the winter on the stems. If you see that the leaves have been infected again in the spring, cut them off and throw them in the organic waste container. From May to mid-July, you can spray an environmentally friendly agent based on organic fatty acids once every two weeks.

Roses that have been affected so badly that they've become bare can be cut down low to three or four branches that still have three or four buds. Give the rose 40-50 grams of organic rose fertiliser. The rose will sprout again and bloom in a month or two.

Precautions: Don't pour water onto the leaves. And make sure to fertilise the plants regularly with organic fertiliser for roses.

THRIPS

Thrips are sap suckers. The female thrips lay their eggs in the tissue of leaves, flower petals or soft stem parts. The larvae of these insects crawl into the bud and eat the tissue of the petals.

Features: The leaves get a drab or greyish-white discolouration. The flowers become damaged and deformed, with brown edges to the petals.

Treatment: Slow-release sachets against thrips. The slow-release sachets contain predatory mites that spread across the plant and eat the thrips eggs and young larvae. After five weeks, the slow-release sachet wears off and you need to hang new sachets to keep protecting the roses.

Precautions: Thrips love low humidity. So increase the humidity by regularly spraying the shrubs with water.

THE JOY OF
roses

FROM THE
OUTSIDE IN

ROSA 'BARISTA'

Cut roses without fragrance

Cut roses have little or no scent. This is because the key aspect in these roses is shelf life. The strength of the fragrance is partly determined by the amount of moisture in the petals. But that moisture causes the flowers to get damaged more easily, which is not helpful for flowers that need to reach their destination unscathed after a lengthy journey. Highly fragrant roses also open sooner, and that doesn't help the shelf life either.

From the outside in

Roses are 'versatile': they work just as well for natural bouquets as for complex, artistic creations

Roses have so many different shapes and colours that they can be combined perfectly with other flowers. They are what you could call 'versatile': they work just as well for natural bouquets as for complex, artistic creations. That's why they're one of the most popular flowers among florists. The best cut roses are the grandiflora roses because they only have a single flower at the end of a long stalk. But shrub and bush roses also make good cut roses.

CUT ROSES

Cut roses are grown mainly in the southern hemisphere, in countries such as Ethiopia, Kenya, Chile, Colombia and Ecuador. From there they are sent to Europe and America to be sold. Sometimes they are in transport for over a week, so they are bred for a long shelf life in addition to their appearance. And they are indeed long-lasting, thanks to petals that are so thick and sturdy that they keep their shape for two to three weeks. That's why most cut roses have little or no fragrance.

From the 1990s, cut rose cultivation declined sharply in both the Netherlands and Belgium. In the Netherlands, the number of cut rose growers dropped from 770 in 2000 to 120 in 2015, and Belgium also saw a big decline. The main reason is the high cost of production in Europe. That's why many companies moved their cut rose cultivation to African and South American countries, where the wages and energy costs are much lower. Around 2015, the cut flower sector in Kenya received negative publicity due to poor working conditions, excess use of scarce water and working with pesticides and the associated damage to the environment. On some flowers, ten different pesticides were found. In response, a covenant was signed in 2019 in which the Dutch flower sector promised to make the cultivation more sustainable. Increasing the wages of the workers at nurseries to an acceptable level was also discussed.

PICKING ROSES

With their sturdy stems, grandiflora roses are suitable for picking and using in bouquets. The white flowers of 'Pascali' have a cream-coloured heart. They don't have much of a scent, but they are resistant to diseases and can cope with rainstorms. Another good rose for picking is 'Ghita Renaissance', a bush rose or low climbing rose (1.5m at most) with highly fragrant pink flowers. The shrub rose 'Peace' blooms with large, yellow-pink flowers that smell nice. 'Blue Girl' has aromatic flowers in an unusual mauve colour. 'Beverly' has very full pink flowers, while those of 'Ingrid Bergman' are dark red and keep well. If you prefer a varied wildflower bouquet, you can choose the English Austin roses. They are a bit more natural.

2.

1.

Rose country

India is the country with the biggest rose production in the world. A lot of varieties specific to India are grown there. After India, China has the largest acreage of roses. Both countries mainly grow roses for their own use; only a small proportion is for export..

Tip for cut roses in a vase

Not every rose is suitable for putting in a vase. Most roses with single flowers are best left in the garden. They lose their petals so quickly when in a vase that you'll soon be left with a bare stem. You can enjoy a fresh bouquet for at least ten days if you take care of it properly:

— Use a clean vase, preferably made of glass. Earthenware vases have pores that can trap bacteria.
— Cut the roses early in the morning or in the evening with a sharp knife. But don't cut them too short because they won't have enough leaves then.
— Cut a few centimetres diagonally off the stem, to open the veins for absorbing water.
— Add a splash of cut flower food (or chlorine and sugar) to the vase. This enhances the shelf life of the roses.
— Fill the vase with tepid water.
— Make sure the leaves aren't in the water. Leaves release toxins into the water, causing the flowers to wilt faster.
— Change the water when it gets cloudy. Cut off a piece off the stalks diagonally each time.
— Keep the vase away from vegetables and fruit, because the ethylene gas they release damages the roses.
— Don't put the bouquet in direct sunlight, near the radiator or near the air conditioning.
— Remove faded flowers so that they can't infect the other flowers.

THE JOY OF

roses

THE FUTURE
FOR ROSES

ALEXANDER ADRIAENSSEN

STILL LIFE WITH FLOWERS IN A GLASS VASE (1650)

ROSES CULTIVATED FROM
CUTTINGS IN A ROSE FIELD IN
NORTH LIMBURG: *ROSA* 'SENSUAL'
(LEFT), *ROSA* 'JAM-A-LICIOUS'
(MIDDLE) AND *ROSA* 'ESPRESSO'
(RIGHT). THE CUTTINGS WERE
PLANTED LATE APRIL/EARLY MAY
AND ALREADY FLOWERING IN JUNE
OF THE SAME YEAR

The future for roses

The breeders listen to what we want and that drives new developments

Roses are constantly changing. Plant breeders make sure of that. They are eager to satisfy our every wish because the money we spend on roses is what keeps the sector alive. In the past, the focus was on the beauty of the bloom. Then roses were bred that were able to cope with diseases better. But people then started to complain that modern roses had lost their fragrance, so breeders such as David Austin started to create roses that not only looked good but smelled lovely too. When reports started to appear about declining bee populations, the demand increased for roses that attract bees. But because bees can't cope with roses that have been treated with chemical pesticides, we demanded roses that are resilient enough to survive without such aids. That is why stronger varieties have appeared on the market recently that can survive without being sprayed. That is a promising development, and fortunately one that is likely to continue.

Smaller gardens

Meanwhile, gardens are becoming smaller due to the lack of land for building homes on. More and more people will have to make do with an apartment that only has at most a window box for roses. If they are lucky enough to have a balcony or roof terrace, they could put some long-flowering roses in pots. That is why breeding companies are working hard on creating mini-roses and micro-roses in a wide range of shapes and colours. For people with small gardens, breeding companies might consider developing roses that mainly grow upwards but need less room than a standard climbing rose.

Climate change

Is that all rose breeders need to consider? No, because for the past few years they have had to take account of the problem of climate change. Because of this, we now want them to come up with roses that can cope with extreme heat, droughts and sudden downpours. Oh, and don't forget the new diseases and pests working their way northwards as temperatures rise in Northern Europe.

The increasing warmth makes it quite likely that people in countries that have been home to roses for centuries will no longer be able to grow the same plants. Nurserymen will have to move to areas with a more rose-friendly climate. What is more, they will need to seek out varieties that are resistant to prolonged drought. It is also conceivable that more advanced techniques will be developed to save water.

Resistance

Like other plants, roses are susceptible to diseases and pests. Chemical protection agents are usually used to combat them, but this approach conflicts with the increasing demand for sustainably produced products. That is why something needs to change if we want to continue buying bunches of roses with a clear conscience. In the past few decades, research has been conducted around the world—including by scientists at Wageningen University in the

1. *ROSA* 'EXOTIC MELLA'
2. ROSES CULTIVATED FROM CUTTINGS OF *ROSA* 'JAM-A-LICIOUS'

Netherlands—on how to breed roses that are resistant to mildew, rose black spot disease and *Agrobacterium*. Roses are selected with the right genes for desirable properties, such as a certain colour, long-lasting as a cut flower in a vase, a stronger scent or resistance to disease. Once the genetic basis for resistance to a disease has been determined, DNA markers can be developed that make plants resistant to these diseases. Correlating the marker profile of a set of plants against measurement data on the plants in the field makes it possible to identify the most promising plants. That reduces the need for time-consuming field trials.

Similarly, research is being carried out to determine which rose species can grow well from their own roots, which would avoid the need for the labour-intensive bud grafting process. Cuttings can be taken from roses with strong roots of their own. Once they have sprouted roots, they can go to the rose nursery where they are grown further.

Coconut fibre substrate

Another new development is that large nurseries, which currently grow most of their plants in soil, are likely to increasingly switch to growing their plants in coconut fibre substrate.

Locally grown

Just as there is an increasing demand for fruit and vegetables that are locally grown, we can expect to see more and more customers wanting roses that have been cultivated locally. After all, that does save on transport costs. Demand for locally cultivated roses could lead to more small nurseries selling their roses in the local market. "Those nurseries are highly likely to grow their roses organically," says rose cultivator Steven van Dalen. "I expect to see rising demand for that in the near future."

1.

2.

"WE LOOK OUT FOR THE LATEST TRENDS SO THAT WE CAN ALWAYS BE ONE STEP AHEAD"

Jessica Keet

FLOWER ARRANGER

Jessica Keet is a multi-talented woman. She acts as a consultant to flower fairs and also is also hired to design company stands for such fairs. "I start with the design and show it to the client. Then the stand is built and I make or hire the decor. Once the supplies of water and electricity have been connected up and the floor laid, I set up the stand. I arrange the flowers and put them in water. I water the plants during the trade fair and clear everything up at the end." In addition to providing input for flower fairs, she also creates bouquets. "I come up with the entire concept. It all depends on what I have been hired to do."

Jessica has seen bouquets change over the course of time. "The style used to be neat and simple, along Biedermeier lines. A bouquet would consist of flowers with short stems, combining to form a tight semicircle. There was also a period with really minimalist bouquets. Since the pandemic, bouquets have gone back to being more exuberant, warmer and inviting. You can tell there is a need for human contact." She often uses bouquets with a mix of flowers of varying stem lengths arranged at different heights.

She doesn't have a favourite rose. "It all depends on what the flower, the bud and the leaf look like. Though I do have a preference for roses with relatively few thorns." The colour doesn't matter either. "As a person, I have my favourite colours—but not in my work. It all depends on what message the client wants to convey. In autumn, I like to use coffee colours and whites, and in spring soft pinks. Of course preferences change, which is why new rose varieties are always appearing. I make sure I keep up with the times and I look out for the latest trends. We see what is coming so we can always be one step ahead."

THE IFTF (INTERNATIONAL FLORICULTURE TRADE FAIR) IN VIJFHUIZEN, THE NETHERLANDS

THE JOY OF
roses

RECIPES

PIERRE AUGUSTE RENOIR
BOUQUET OF ROSES (1882)

Organic
Only use roses that have been grown organically or that you can be sure have not been sprayed with pesticides. Don't pick buds; only use flowers that have opened up.

Use roses of the same variety for any given recipe
Each variety has its own flavour so it is best not to mix different kinds of roses. Rinse the petals thoroughly before use.

The roses with the best flavour
— *Rosa* 'Roseraie de l'Hay'
— Damask rose (*Rosa damascena*)
— Apothecary's rose (*Rosa gallica* 'Officinalis')
— Eglantine (*Rosa rubiginosa*)
— Japanese rose (*Rosa rugosa*)

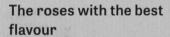

Rose hips
Only pluck ripe rose hips—ones that are deep red and break open easily. The first half of October is a good time for this. But don't wait too long, because otherwise the birds will have them!

Recipes

All roses are edible and you can come up with endless variations

All roses are edible, provided they haven't been sprayed. The stronger the rose's scent, the stronger the flavour. Some roses taste bitter but you can reduce that effect by cutting off the white part where the petal attaches.

Roses are incredibly healthy. Medicinal properties have been attributed to them since time immemorial. The Chinese were already planting them specifically for that purpose some 5000 years ago. In Persia 3000 years ago, dishes were decorated with rose petals. This was followed by the discovery of rosewater, which was used to flavour sweet dishes in Egypt, Greece, Rome, Persia and South-East Asia—and still is today. It takes a thousand kilograms of rose petals to produce one kilogram of rose oil!

It was a while before people in Europe started using roses in food. It was only in the fourteenth century that they started using rosewater in fish and game dishes, sauces, preserved food and desserts. The use of rosewater declined from the mid-eighteenth century onwards as vanilla became cheaper and was used instead. The health-giving benefits of rose petals are evident from the fact that the *Rosa gallica* is also known as the 'apothecary's rose'.

There has been renewed interest in the use of edible flowers in dishes and as decoration in recent years. You can use them in many different ways: in jelly, syrup, oil, butter, vinegar, sugar, rosewater, salt, tea, wine, biscuits and cakes, or as decorations and so on. The rose hips can be turned into jam, syrup, puree, chutney or tea.

The fragrant Damask rose (*Rosa damascena*) has been used for centuries to make rose oil that is then used in perfumes. Turkey, Romania and Bulgaria used to have large nurseries growing these roses. In fact, they still exist in Bulgaria and Turkey.

Potpourri

A potpourri is a mixture of natural, fragrant ingredients such as petals, herbs, citrus peel and spices. Potpourri can be used as decoration and scent in a bowl, vase or basket. Another idea is to put the mixture in little bags that you then hang up in your clothes cupboard.
I have placed them on a paper towel on the window sill. When the sun comes out, they dry even faster. Remove them from the sun once they have dried, though, otherwise they will soon discolour.

MAKE YOUR OWN

Pluck the roses on a dry, sunny day, preferably early in the morning or late in the afternoon when the scent is strongest. Pull off the petals and lay them on a tea towel or paper towel on the window sill. Leave them to dry at room temperature for at least a week. Make sure the petals don't touch one another, as they could otherwise go mouldy. You don't need to turn them over. Remove them from the sun as soon as they have dried, as they will otherwise discolour. Take a large bowl and put the flowers in it, together with fruits, pine cones, herbs, cinnamon sticks, cloves and nutmeg for example.

In a separate dish, mix ground spices with a few drops of scented oil and/or essential oil. Adding orris root powder (or a similar fixative) helps preserve the scents better. Pour this mixture into the bowl with the dried flowers and herbs. Then put it all into a glass jar and seal it so that it is airtight. Leave the jar in a warm, dark spot. Shake it occasionally. The potpourri will be ready after six weeks.

HERBERT JAMES DRAPER:
POTPOURRI (1897)

White, pale pink and yellow petals turn brown, while red petals turn bordeaux red.

Drying petals

The Ancient Romans used rose petals in the bath, as a filling for mattresses and cushions and scattered as decoration for parties. But anything the Romans did, we can do too. You can buy the petals or dry your own. If you want to do it yourself, hang the flowers upside-down in a dark, cool place or put them on the window sill, but not in bright sunlight. Give them enough space to dry properly and leave them hanging for a couple of weeks until they feel dry.

Raining roses

The annual celebration of Mass on Whitsunday is marked by a special tradition in the Pantheon. Rome's fire brigade drops bright red rose petals through the oculus (the hole at the top of the building), which float down, spreading a strong scent of roses throughout the building. This tradition refers to the Pentecostal story that the Holy Spirit appeared to the apostles in the form of flames.

Rosewater made from dried petals

INGREDIENTS

¼ cup dried rose petals

300 ml distilled or filtered water,
   or pure mineral water

ALSO NEEDED

2 preserving jars with large mouths

tea sieve

Rosewater is made from rose petals. Each rose has its own scent and some roses are better suited to making rosewater than others. The best are *Rosa damascena*, *Rosa centifolia* and *Rosa gallica*. The more fragrant the rose, the stronger the scent of the rosewater.

Rosewater is created by distilling the rose petals. The steam releases the essential oils and hydrolates in the plant. Water vapour is created during the distillation process that contains all the plant's soluble components. Rosewater contains vitamins A, B3, C, D and E, as well as antioxidants. As a result, rosewater has an anti-inflammatory effect and it is also good for treating skin impurities.

PREPARATION

— Put the dried rose petals in one jar.
— Boil the water, let it cool a little and pour it on top of the rose petals.
— Close the jar and let the water cool.
— Place the tea sieve over the opening of the second (empty) jar. Pour the cooled rosewater into the jar. The sieve will catch the petals.
— Close the jar and place it in the fridge. The rosewater will keep for a week.

Applications

Rosewater can be used in various ways. Add a few drops and some sprigs of mint to a jug of water. Sprinkle some drops over a fruit salad. Or add some drops to the dough for a cake or biscuits.

Rosewater made from fresh petals

INGREDIENTS

1 cup fresh petals from roses that haven't been sprayed

475 ml distilled or filtered water

ALSO NEEDED

tea sieve

1 large preserving jar

PREPARATION

— Pluck as many rose petals as will fit into a cup. Leave the petals outside for 15 minutes to allow the insects on them to escape.

— Crush the petals, put them in a pan and pour the water over them.

— Warm the pan on a very low heat. Make sure the water doesn't boil.

— Place the sieve over the jar opening and pour the rosewater into the jar. Let the rosewater cool completely.

— Close the jar and put it in the fridge. The rosewater will keep for a week.

Rose drink

INGREDIENTS

½ lime

petals from 2 fresh roses

1 litre mineral water

250 ml tonic water

1 tablespoon rosewater

PREPARATION

— Slice the lime.

— Mix all the ingredients and leave them to infuse for two to three days.

Pink colour

If you use red or purple roses, the drink will have an attractive pink colour.

Rose punch

INGREDIENTS

ice cubes (about three per glass)

1 teaspoon of rosewater

750 ml dry white wine

750 ml sparkling mineral water

fresh rose petals

PREPARATION

— Put the ice cubes in some attractive glasses.

— Add the rosewater, the white wine and the mineral water.

— Decorate the rose punch with rose petals.

Rose jam made from rose petals

INGREDIENTS

the fresh petals of 5-10 roses

200 ml water

300 g semi-sweet gelling sugar

1 tablespoon rose vinegar

1 tablespoon rosewater

ALSO NEEDED

a couple of jam jars

PREPARATION

— Cut the white tips off the rose petals and wash the petals.

— Put the water in a pan.

— Keep adding rose petals until the water just covers them. Leave them overnight to infuse.

— Blend the mixture fine with a hand-held blender. Then bring it to the boil. Add the gelling sugar.

— Once the sugar has dissolved, add the rose vinegar and the rosewater. Boil the mixture until the jam is sufficiently thick. Test this by placing a drop of the jam on a cold dish. The jam should stick to the dish when you turn it upside down.

— Then pour the rose jam into clean jars.

Rose butter

INGREDIENTS

4 or 5 large, fresh roses that have not
   been sprayed
250g butter, at room temperature
salt
white pepper
a touch of curry powder or coriander
   (optional)

PREPARATION

— Wash and dry the rose petals. Cut the white tips off, as they can be bitter.
— Cut the rose petals into very fine strips.
— Beat the butter until it is soft. Then add the rose petals and stir them into the
   butter.
— Add salt and white pepper to taste to the butter.
— Curry powder or coriander can be added if so desired.

This is a savoury accompaniment that you can use like a herb butter. It goes very
well with steak or fried fish, or on bread or toast as an appetiser. It can also be kept
in the freezer.

roses

ROSE SOCIETIES

ÉTIENNE ADOLPHE PIOT
GIRL WITH ROSE BASKET (1910)

Rose societies

If you want to know all about roses, it's useful to become a member of a rose society

The Dutch Rose Society (*Nederlandse Rozenvereniging*) was founded in 1966. The society regularly organises talks and excursions in the Netherlands and abroad for its members. The society has a website with discussions of hot topics and announcements of events and excursions.

Members of the Dutch Rose Society receive a magazine—the *Rozenbulletin*—four times a year. It contains articles about rose gardens and the gardens of rose-growing enthusiasts in addition to the latest news and history facts. Rose growers, botanists and experienced members give their expert opinions on how to plant and care for roses and how to prevent or tackle diseases. All the articles are illustrated with superb photos, of course. The magazine is only available to society members. Membership costs €30 a year for people living in the Netherlands and €35 if you live abroad.

The society has a Facebook page with information about events, plus a separate Facebook group where rose lovers can share their photos and experiences. www.rozenvereniging.nl

There are dozens of national rose societies in other countries too. The World Federation of Rose Societies is the overarching organisation uniting rose societies in 39 countries. Some of its members are:

— **Belgium**
   Société Royale Nationale 'Les Amis de la Rose'/Koninklijke Nationale Maatschappij 'De Vrienden van de Roos'. Founded in 1926.
   www.rosabelgica.be
— **Germany**
   Deutsche Rosengesellschaft e.V. Founded in 1883.
   www.rosengesellschaft.de
— **France**
   Société Française des Roses 'Les Amis des Roses'. Founded in 1896.
   www.societefrancaisedesroses.asso.fr
— **UK**
   Rose Society UK. Founded in 2017.
   www.therosesociety.org.uk

A HEDGE OF
ROSA 'LILL LINDFORS'

"UNFORTUNATELY I DON'T HAVE A LARGE COUNTRY ESTATE WITH A SPOT FOR EVERY ROSE"

Marnix Bakker

ACTIVE MEMBER
OF THE DUTCH ROSE SOCIETY

"As a child, I was always pottering in the garden with all the plants and beasties, although my mother noticed I'd mainly be doing things with the roses. The reason I got so involved in roses later on was because of the scents. And a rose I discovered in the front garden twenty years ago. My wife and I had just moved to the village of Kropswolde. The facade of our new house had a rose growing up it. I thought it was probably a very old one. And I was right—it turned out to be a rose from the seventeenth century! I immediately joined the Dutch Rose Society and asked them if they knew what kind of a rose it was. Finding out the name of an unknown rose proved to be quite a difficult task. Members of the Rose Society took photos and a description of my rose with them on a rose-themed trip to England. It turned out that the rose, a *Rosa* x *centifolia*, used to be used as a buttonhole in England in the past.

I have always enjoyed writing and in 2005 I was asked whether I would like to write for the *Rozenbulletin*, the Dutch Rose Society's magazine. My first article was about dark rambler roses. Pretty much every article I wrote involved buying a rose as I would get so interested in the rose I was investigating, or the story behind it, that I would want to try it out in my own garden. I also planted the roses I

was writing about in a garden that I laid out for someone else (because unfortunately I don't have a large country estate with a spot for every rose). When I purchase a rose, I often haven't decided where I'm going to put it. I plant it somewhere and then replant it in the autumn because it doesn't grow as I expected it to.

I don't usually join in the excursions organised by the Dutch Rose Society. In that sense I'm a bit unusual. I'm more the kind of person to take his mother on a drive in a vintage Renault Quatrelle. Then we'll sit on a bench in a rose garden eating muesli bars we brought with us.

The Society's rose excursions are much more luxury than that. You would expect the people going on those trips to be mainly interested in learning a lot about roses. But that's not the case; for them it's mostly a social occasion. The weird thing is that all rose society members the world over are like that. I once went to an international rose convention in Denmark, with rose lovers from all over the world. People were networking, drinking coffee, eating cake and chatting away. But when the organisers asked who wanted to go on a field trip to be told more about the new rose seedlings and the selection process used by the rose grower who was featured that day, my mother and I were

the only people interested. I don't really know why that is. The Dutch Rose Society invites speakers to its members' meetings, and those are often fascinating talks. We also have a Facebook page that I manage. The members are mainly older people; there aren't many youngsters. You reach a different crowd through Facebook. Young people have very different expectations from a society. They aren't interested in annual general meetings and minutes. They are more focused on what they can do in their gardens; they want practical tips. If they see a photo on Facebook of a rose they like the look of, they ask me how much I want for it. Apparently they think the rose society people run a rose nursery.

There are a lot of roses I like but I definitely have my favourites. I find an attractive scent important. *Rosa sericea* var. *omeiensis* 'Hidcote Gold' is one of my favourites. It

has yellow flowers, it has inherited the honey scent of a *Rosa hugonis* and the amazing thorns of the *Rosa sericea* f. *pteracantha*. I've been working on breeding roses with such impressive thorns for decades now. And yes, I have finally managed it. The next step is to get a different colour in the flowers, because they have all been yellow so far. In 2011, I grew a moss rose by combining two rose groups in one plant: moss roses and rugosa roses. This *Rosa* 'Rugged Moss' is very healthy and can be planted as a shrub or guided as a climber. The open flowers are popular with insects.

In the Winschoten rose garden, I'm part of the team that does the inspections. We monitor the roses for several successive years. We note the scores per person and hand in the results. Up to five or so years ago, the inspections didn't include the scent; that wasn't an item on the forms. The focus was on the rose's state of health. But fortunately

the scent is now back as one of the criteria. You can assess the scent in terms of how strong it is. You can also train yourself to distinguish different scents by comparing them and reading descriptions. You might see 'smell of cloves' for example. There are also roses that smell of apples or bananas. I described one rose as smelling of chicken soup. My mother said I shouldn't use that description but it's the linseed oil that reminds me of chicken soup. That oil holds the scent, like the alcohol does in eau de cologne.

I give pruning courses in the Winschoten rose garden. People often have this idea that pruning is complicated. I help them to get over their fear and persuade them to cut low down. The people on the course often have a tendency to cut the young long shoots rather than the old woody branches. Then all you are doing is topping it and the shrub ages even more. You need to prune the rose to activate it. If it is already active, you don't need to prune it at all. In my garden I have trained the 'Little Gem' moss rose over a rose arch. So my 'Little Gem' isn't so little at all any more. But how do you encourage it to grow like that? Answer: by binding the rose, sawing off the old branches and *not* pruning the young shoots."

2.

1. WINSCHOTEN ROSE GARDEN
2. *ROSA* 'LITTLE GEM'

THE JOY OF
roses

ROSE GARDENS

THE ROSE GARDEN
AT AMERONGEN CASTLE

Rose gardens

Rose gardens were created to promote roses, aimed at the 'man in the street'

ROSE GARDENS IN THE NETHERLANDS

The first rose gardens in the Netherlands were laid out in the second half of the nineteenth century. They were attached to castles and country estates. Later, country houses and detached suburban houses got their own rose gardens, to be followed by public parks. The rose garden at Castle Weldam in Diepenheim is the oldest Dutch rose garden in the mixed garden style. It was designed by Hugo Poortman in 1886. He went on to create rose gardens in Amerongen (1889), Middachten in De Steeg (1901), Twickel in Ambt Delden (1907), Huis Doorn (1910) and Warmelo in Diepenheim (1927).

On 10 November 1891, rose lovers founded the Society for the Promotion of Rose Growing, naming it 'Nos Jungunt Rosae' ('we are united by roses'). One of the society's objectives was to create rose gardens and thereby spread the love of roses among the general public. In 1913, the society's members reserved 1,000 square metres for the creation of a rose garden in the Hogelandse Park, which had just been laid out in Utrecht. The rose garden was opened on 7 June 1913, making it the first rose garden to be open to the public in the Netherlands. And to show vanity is a universal characteristic, three borders next to the entrance were planted with shrub roses that were given the names of members of the Nos Jungunt Rosae board. The middle border had the dark red rose 'Mrs Dora van Tets', named after the secretary's wife. To the right was a border with 'Sir J.L. Mock', the society chairman. Planted in the border on the left was 'Veluwezoom', a rose cultivated by the deputy chairman M.J. Baron van Pallandt.

The next public rose garden was created shortly afterwards at the Peace Palace in The Hague. In 1914, Nos Jungunt Rosae laid out their own society rose garden, called Sonsbeek, in Arnhem but it had to close just one year later due to financial problems. Amersfoort got a rose garden in 1914, to be followed by the cities of Meppel (1929), Venlo (1929), Rotterdam (1931) and Hengelo (1931). The Netherlands' largest rose garden was laid out in the Vondelpark in Amsterdam in 1936. Ten of the society's thirteen projects have survived. Sonsbeek, Soestdijk and Naarden have gone. Amersfoort's rose garden was turned into a playground after 1945 but that no longer exists. However, a new rose garden was planted in Amersfoort's Park Schothorst in 2005.

Utrecht's rose garden was completely renovated about twenty years ago, while keeping the original layout almost intact. In the centre of the garden stands a fountain in the shape of a pomegranate.

Eighteen of the 63 rose borders in Amsterdam's Vondelpark got a make-over in 2016. Amsterdam municipality carried out the major work such as raising the soil level and preparing the borders for planting. The rose garden is maintained by volunteers from the Hart voor het Vondelpark foundation.

OUDWIJK ROSE GARDEN IN THE
HOGELANDSE PARK IN UTRECHT

THERE IS A HERITAGE ROUTE
STARTING IN THE ROSE GARDEN.
SCAN THE QR CODE FOR MORE
INFORMATION

LIST OF ROSE GARDENS IN THE NETHERLANDS, BELGIUM, GERMANY AND THE UK

Rose gardens in the Netherlands

Aalsmeer: Horticultural Museum and Historical Garden

Amerongen: Amerongen Castle gardens

Amsterdam: Rosarium Vondelpark

Barneveld: De Beukenhof

Boskoop: Rosarium Guldemondplantsoen

Bussum: Het Gooise Land

De Steeg: Middachten Castle, rose garden

Doorn: Huis Doorn Museum rose garden

The Hague: Westbroekpark rose garden

Kats: In de Zeeuwse Oase (was Zeeland Rose Garden)

Leiden: Hortus Botanicus rose garden

Lottum: Rosarium and the Rozenhof

Neerijnen: Neerijnen Castle gardens

Oostkapelle: the Romantic Rose Garden

Rotterdam: the rose garden in Plaswijckpark

Utrecht: Rosarium Oudwijk

Venlo: Rosarium

Vorden: De Wiersse

Wageningen: Belmonte Arboretum

Winschoten: Rosarium

Rose gardens in Belgium

Antwerpen: Antwerp, Rivierenhof rose garden

Bergen: Havré Castle rose garden

Brasschaat: rose garden in the municipal park

Bruges: rose garden in Paradisio 'Brugelette' park

Kortrijk: Kortrijk International Rose Garden

Malmedy: Daniel Schmitz Rose Garden

Mechelen: rose garden in Vrijbroekpark

Opbeek: Rosarium-Lensarium

Oudenburg: rose garden belonging to Lens Roses nursery

Putte: Casteels rose garden and nursery

Saint-Hubert: Rosarium Pierre Joseph Redouté

Sint-Pieters-Leeuw: Coloma rose garden

Rose gardens in Germany

Bad Kissingen: Rosengarten
Dortmund: Westfalenpark
Eppelborn-Dirmingen: Freizeitzentrum Finkenrech (recreational centre)
Hadamar: Rosengarten
Lake Constance: Mainau Island
Ludwigsburg: Ludwigsburg Palace
Mannheim: Luisenpark
Mannheim: rose garden in Herzogenriedpark
Sangerhausen: Europa Rosarium (was Rosarium Sangerhausen). Has the largest collection of roses in the world with 80,000 plants
Steinfurth: Rosenpark Dräger
Zweibrücken: Zweibrücken rose garden

Rose gardens in the UK

Albrighton: The David Austin Rose Gardens
Alcester: Coughton Court
Alnwick: the Alnwick Garden
Attleborough: Peter Beales Roses
Balerno: Malleny Garden
Chipping Campden: Kiftsgate Court Gardens
Cranbrook: Sissinghurst Castle Garden
Englefield: the Savill Garden
Haywards Heath: Borde Hill

London: Queen Mary's Gardens in Regent's Park
Richmond: Royal Botanic Gardens, Kew
Romsey: Mottisfont Abbey Rose Garden
St. Albans: Gardens of the Rose
Stowmarket: Helmington Hall Gardens
Westerham: Chartwell
Winchcombe: Sudeley Castle & Gardens
Windsor: Windsor Great Park
Wolverhampton: Wightwick Manor
York: Castle Howard Estate

National collections of historic roses are held in several locations. Below is a selection:

Pre-1900 roses: Mottisfont Abbey Rose Garden, Romsey
Pemberton and Bentall roses: St Francis Hospice, Havering-atte-Bower
Species and old roses: Peter Beales Roses, Attleborough
Rambling roses: Moor Wood, Woodmancote
Pre-1900 gallica's: Carolside, Earlston
Species and older hybrid roses: Malleny Garden, Balerno

"THEY DO TEN TO FIFTEEN MILLION ROSES A YEAR, SO YOU NEED A LOT OF PEOPLE FOR THAT"

Sabine, Tjeu, Tineke, Eugenie and Marianne

VOLUNTEERS
AT THE ROZENHOF IN LOTTUM

If you are a rose lover, you will adore the rose village of Lottum. To get there, you drive past endless fields of roses and marigolds, making you realise this is a place that revolves around the Queen of Flowers. At the heart of the village of Lottum, in Limburg in the southern Netherlands, is the Rozenhof. This rose garden is home to 375 different species of roses. If you want to know more about them, you can get a guided tour (available May to November). The guide will also take you to the museum with its exhibition about the history and future of roses. And if you still have questions after that, you can visit the Knowledge Centre with shelves full of books, which you can leaf through on the patio with its views of the rose garden, while you enjoy a cup of coffee or tea. Of course Rozenhof has its own gift shop where you can purchase rose-themed gifts ranging from decorated coffee mugs to rose jam and rose beer. Keep an eye on their calendar so you know when the gardens open for the season and when the dates are for rose tasting, rose recipe workshops and the Rose Festival.

How did Lottum end up as a rose village? Why is it that 70 per cent of all shrub roses grown in the Netherlands—15 million plants a year!—come from here? To find out, I spoke to five villagers who work as volunteers at the Rozenhof.

Sabine van de Laak is a graphic designer and provides the Rozenhof with cards, folders and booklets she designed herself. Tjeu in 't Zandt has delved into the history of Lottum. Tineke van den Brandt, Eugenie Breukers and Marianne van der Heijden give guided tours of the Rozenhof. We start by running through some historical facts. It turns out Lottum ended up with its roses by pure chance. More specifically, thanks to a curate named Frans Lichtevelt who was appointed to Lottum in 1817. He was sickly and a doctor recommended a visit to the French spa town of Vichy. The surrounding area had a lot of tree nurseries and to pass the time, Frans began learning about how to grow fruit trees. When he returned to Lottum in 1830, he shared his new knowledge with various fellow villagers. Keen to earn some extra money, they dedicated part of their land to growing fruit trees. In around 1850, the locals discovered that, like fruit trees, roses could be propagated using bud grafting. Lottum's tree growers had plenty of experience of this technique by then with their fruit trees, so they added roses to their plots. Roses had many advantages: they took up less room than the trees, they produced income more quickly than the fruit, and all you needed to grow them was a trowel, a budding knife and a hoe. This soon turned out to

be a smart move because roses were becoming increasingly popular with the growing prosperity. Lottum got its own train station in 1883, which made it easier to transport the roses to customers.

"The people of Lottum started cultivating roses seriously in around 1900," explains Tjeu. "You didn't need anything: you just bought half a dozen plants and got going." Lottum's rose

1. THE ROSES IN THE ROSE GARDEN HAVE NOT BEEN SPRAYED AND YOU MAY TRY A TASTE OF ANY OF THEM
2. *ROSA* 'ISN'T SHE BEAUTIFUL'
3. GUIDED TOUR OF THE GARDEN

growers would go to their fields, says Eugenie, "And between 12 and 1 o'clock they would go home for lunch—that break was sacred. But after the evening meal, they would return to the field to cut the bud grafts. In my day, women worked in the fields too."

Tineke knows all about that. She may not have been born in Lottum, but she married a Lottum rose grower in 1976. "When I moved here, there were about two thousand inhabitants and some sixty nurseries. Actually, there were more than that because the grower's son would often start growing roses as a separate business. There were also a lot of mixed businesses that grew asparagus or mushrooms in addition to the roses. Most people in Lottum run their own business; they are hard-working folk. They are very forthright, because everyone decides for themselves what they are going to do and how. You have to make sure you have buyers for your products. You grow the flowers and you determine how to sell them. That's why no one ever managed to set up a grower's association here: it was every man for himself."

Children would start bud grafting in the final year of primary school, for half the day at first. These days you're paid per rose, but back then the wages depended on your age. "Youngsters work quickly," says Sabine. "Young people earned a lot of money from this work. Lottum's young people always had plenty of cash." Tjeu was one of them. "You'd have a thousand pieces of grafting tape in one bag," he says. "In 1963, you got ten guilders when your bag was empty, meaning you'd used all your tape. We would work in pairs. The grower would make the graft in the lower stem and I'd stick the tape around it. Growers could make up to 3000 grafts a day."

This work is still done by hand, says Tineke. "They do ten to fifteen million roses a year, so you need a lot of people for that. We start bud grafting in early June and continue through to August. After then you don't get any more growth, the bark doesn't open up. It is labour-intensive with low margins."

You can't plant new roses in a spot that was previously used to grow roses. "In the past you would have to wait five years. But there were so many growers here who needed the land that it was difficult to find new plots. So about thirty years ago they started disinfecting the soil to get rid of nematodes. When that was no longer allowed because of the toxins, it was discovered that marigolds (*Tagetes*) have the same effect." Once or twice a year, the Rozenhof organises a tasting of

Pull rather than cut

Tineke: "Suckers should be pulled off rather than cut off. If you cut them, there is always a bit left behind, which has eyes. They turn into buds and before you know it you have five shoots."

Hedge trimmer

Tineke: "Pruning roses is perfectly simple. Hybrid tea roses—shrubs with one rose per branch—have to be pruned back to the third bud eye. With climbing roses, I cut off old branches at the base. That will produce a new shoot, which I then train. That rejuvenates the shrub. I use a hedge trimmer for all other types of roses. I trim them almost to the base, then remove spindly stems and dead wood. It sounds brutal, but the roses are fine with this treatment."

edible roses. During this event, visitors can nibble rose petals and make rose vinegar and rose butter. That the Rozenhof has so many activities on offer is thanks to Betty Kranz, who unfortunately passed away in 2019. "She was so enthusiastic, she infected us all with her love of roses," says Tineke. "She trained us as tour guides. I've lived here for forty-five years, I'm married to a rose grower and I've grafted thousands of the plants but beyond that I didn't know anything about roses. For example, I never knew you could eat them! I'm still amazed by that. Roses are incredibly healthy. One flower has as many antioxidants as 250 blueberries. The darker the rose, the more nutrients it contains. And did you know rose hips have almost six times as much vitamin C by weight as kiwis?" "The people of Lottum reckon they know everything there is to know about roses," laughs Marianne, "but when they come here and hear our stories, they are amazed."

DE ROZENHOF
Markt 2, 5973 NR Lottum, Netherlands.
Opening hours: May-October daily 10 a.m.–5 p.m.;
winter opening on Sundays 1.30 p.m.–4.30 p.m.
www.rozenhoflottum.nl

WEBSITES EN
ADDRESSES

Websites and addresses

General
en.wikipedia.org/wiki/List_of_rose_breeders
www.helpmefind.com/roses
www.rhs.org.uk/plants/roses/choosing-the-best

UK
www.therosesociety.org.uk (The Rose Society UK)
eu.davidaustinroses.com
www.fryersroses.co.uk/roses
www.thesmellofroses.com
www.trevorwhiteroses.co.uk
www.warnersroses.com

Ireland
www.rosesocietyni.com (The Rose Society of Northern Ireland)
www.eplantsireland.com

USA
www.rose.org (American Rose Society)
www.allmythyme.com
www.jacksonandperkins.com
www.rosenotes.com

the Netherlands
www.rozenvereniging.nl (Dutch Rose Society)
www.kwekerijennederland.nl

Belgium
www.rozenvrienden.be (Belgian Rose Society)
www.rozenkring.be (Belgian Rose Society)
www.derozenkring.be
www.mooietuinen.be/rozentuinen.html
www.plantenkwekerijen.be/nederlandserozen.html

ROSA 'GARDEN OF ROSES'

INDEX

Page numbers in bold face refer to pictures.

PHOTO CREDITS

p. 25 (1, 2, 3) Jacques Verschuren Fotografie

p. 49 (3) Rose nursery De Wilde

p. 57 (5), p. 81 (1), p. 83 (1), p. 97 (5, 8), p. 111 (5), p. 117 (1), p. 124 (3), p. 152, p. 174, p. 177 (2) Jan Spek Rozen

p. 83 (2), p. 197 (1, 2), p. 199 (2) Marnix Bakker

p. 88-89, p. 182 (below centre), p. 191, p. 209 (1) Sabine Kamp-Bosman

p. 91 Lei Spreeuwenberg

p. 94, p. 97 (1, 2, 3, 4,7) Martin Vissers

p. 111 Laura Muijsers, Royal Plant Rosarium Lottum BV

p. 119 Fridtjof Bremer

p. 120 Martje van den Bosch

p. 125 Adobe Stock / hhelene

p. 141 (1, 2) and p. 142 (1) Modeste Herwig

p. 147 (1, 2) Roger Willeghems

p. 178 Arie Palsgraaf

p. 179 Jessica Keet

p. 196 Kitty Karis

p. 208 Janneke in 't Zandt-Kleuskens

Photos p. 90 with the cooperation of Toon de Rijk, www.rozenrijk.nl

Recipes p. 187, p. 188, p. 189, p. 190, p. 191 with thanks to Sabine Kamp-Bosman and the Rozenhof in Lottum

PHOTO LOCATIONS

p. 104 Woolstone Mill House, Faringdon, Oxfordshire, UK

p. 136 Hanneke and René Vermeulen, Amersfoort. Private garden

p. 137 (3) Lime Close Garden, Abingdon, Oxfordshire, UK

p. 139 (large photo) Tuin Erf Klein Rassert, Hoevelaken, www.erfkleinrassert.jouwweb.nl

IN THIS SERIES

Liefde voor rozen
ISBN 978 90 8989 953 8

The Joy of Roses
ISBN 978 90 8989 991 0

Liefde voor dahlia's
ISBN 978 90 5837 105 8

The Joy of Dahlias
ISBN 978 90 8989 825 8

CREDITS

© 2024 TERRA publishers
Uitgeverij Terra is part of TerraLannoo bv
P.O. Box 23202
1100 DS Amsterdam
the Netherlands

info@terralannoo.nl
www.terra-publishing.com

 terrapublishing
 terrapublishing

Text: Nicolien van Doorn
English translation: Tessera Translations SL (Mike and Clare Wilkinson, Mariëlle Kakebeen)
Photography cover and interior: Anneke Beemer Tuin & Fotografie
Editing: Barbara Luijken en Marijke Overpelt
Index: Trijnie Duut
Design cover and interior: The Creative Rebels, Sabrina Raams

First print, 2024

ISBN 978 90 8989 991 0
NUR 424, 421